"C. S. Lewis famously observed, 'If you read history you will find that the Christians who did most for the present world were those who thought most of the next.'" Our problem is not that we think too much about heaven but rather think too little of it. In *A Place Called Heaven*, my friend Robert Jeffress has done a masterful job of helping believers think biblically about that future home Jesus is preparing for every believer."

Dr. David Jeremiah, founder and president,
Turning Point Ministries

"When it comes to the bottom line for Christians, heaven is it. Our life on earth is but a brief wisp of vapor compared to the eternity of heaven, so it makes sense to learn as much as possible about our everlasting home. Dr. Jeffress does a stellar job of answering peoples' questions about this marvelous place beyond our tombstones, and I highly recommend *A Place Called Heaven* to every Christ-follower. I also recommend it to those who do not yet follow Christ, as it will give the skeptical reader solid, biblical answers to their toughest questions about the world beyond the grave!"

Joni Eareckson Tada, Joni and Friends
International Disability Center

"We're all curious about heaven, and thankfully this book uses biblical teaching to enable us to get a peek behind the curtain. Read it to be reminded that the best is yet to come!"

Dr. Erwin W. Lutzer, pastor emeritus,
The Moody Church, Chicago, Illinois

"Why is it that most of us know so little about heaven? If how we live here directly impacts how we live there—in eternity—shouldn't we know more about the consequences of this life and about the place God is preparing for His heirs? I'm so excited about this book you hold in your hands. Dr. Jeffress is a strong Christian voice in this day of chaos. And *A Place Called Heaven* is a clarion call for us all to look up and consider afresh how much God loves us and how profoundly our lives on earth matter. Jesus is preparing a place in heaven for you, a place that fits you perfectly. Imagine! May you devour these pages, as I did, and begin to live more purposefully with eternity in mind."

Susie Larson, talk radio host, national speaker, and author of *Your Powerful Prayers*

"Robert Jeffress gets right to the point—in fact, he gets to ten of the main points people need to know and believe if they expect to go to heaven. *A Place Called Heaven* is clear and biblical in its approach. This is a good read for all and a great tool to use in sharing the good news of the gospel with others."

Dr. Mark L. Bailey, president, Dallas Theological Seminary, Dallas, Texas

"A thousand years from today you will be alive . . . somewhere. No one is really ready to live life to the fullest until he or she is ready to die. Robert Jeffress opens biblical truth with the desired end that you can have the assurance you will live forever in . . . *A Place Called Heaven*."

Dr. O. S. Hawkins, president/CEO, GuideStone Financial Resources, Dallas, Texas

"Dr. Robert Jeffress not only continues to have one of the most remarkable preaching ministries in America but also makes it available through the publication of many of those messages. The present book on heaven is no exception. The vast majority seem to fear preaching on eternal destiny and are much more moved by the social agendas of the day. But *A Place Called Heaven* answers serious questions that the average believer desperately wants to know. Further, this tome will generate a desire on the part of those who read it to experience for themselves the glories of heaven. The chapter on what people will do in heaven is one of the most perceptive I have ever read."

Dr. Paige Patterson, president, Southwestern Baptist Theological Seminary, Ft. Worth, Texas

A PLACE CALLED
HEAVEN

10 Surprising Truths about Your Eternal Home

DR. ROBERT
JEFFRESS

BakerBooks

a division of Baker Publishing Group
Grand Rapids, Michigan

Published by Baker Books
a division of Baker Publishing Group
P.O. Box 6287, Grand Rapids, MI 49516-6287
www.bakerbooks.com

Printed in the United States of America

Library of Congress Cataloging-in-Publication Data
Names: Jeffress, Robert, 1955– author.
Title: A place called heaven : 10 surprising truths about your eternal home / Dr. Robert Jeffress.
Description: Grand Rapids, MI : Baker Books, 2017. | Includes bibliographical references.
Identifiers: LCCN 2017009763 | ISBN 9780801018947 (cloth) | ISBN 9780801076961 (ITPE)
Subjects: LCSH: Heaven—Christianity—Miscellanea.
Classification: LCC BT846.3 .J44 2017 | DDC 236/.24—dc23
LC record available at https://lccn.loc.gov/2017009763

Unless otherwise indicated, Scripture quotations are from the New American Standard Bible®, Copyright © 1960, 1962, 1963, 1968, 1971, 1972, 1973, 1975, 1977, 1995 by The Lockman Foundation. Used by permission. (www.Lockman.org)

Scripture quotations labeled NIV are from the Holy Bible, New International Version®. NIV®. Copyright © 1973, 1978, 1984, 2011 by Biblica, Inc.™ Used by permission of Zondervan. All rights reserved worldwide. www.zondervan.com

Scripture quotations labeled NKJV are from the New King James Version®. Copyright © 1982 by Thomas Nelson, Inc. Used by permission. All rights reserved.

Scripture quotations labeled NLT are from the *Holy Bible*, New Living Translation, copyright © 1996, 2004, 2015 by Tyndale House Foundation. Used by permission of Tyndale House Publishers, Inc., Carol Stream, Illinois 60188. All rights reserved.

Scripture quotations labeled Phillips are from The New Testament in Modern English, revised edition—J. B. Phillips, translator. © J. B. Phillips 1958, 1960, 1972. Used by permission of Macmillan Publishing Co., Inc.

Scripture quotations labeled TLB are from The Living Bible, copyright © 1971. Used by permission of Tyndale House Publishers, Inc., Carol Stream, Illinois 60188. All rights reserved.

All italics in Scripture quotations are the author's emphasis.

Published in association with Yates & Yates, www.yates2.com.

17 18 19 20 21 22 23   7 6 5

To Randy and Kathie King

Thank you for your vision
for our Pathway to Victory ministry
as we share with the world
the message of Jesus Christ—the only Way
to that "place called heaven."

Contents

Acknowledgments

No book is a solo effort. I'm deeply indebted to the following people who were tremendously helpful in creating and communicating this encouraging message about "a place called heaven."

Brian Vos, Mark Rice, Brianna DeWitt, Lindsey Spoolstra, and the entire team at Baker Books, who caught the vision for this book immediately.

Derrick G. Jeter, our creative director at Pathway to Victory, who was an invaluable help to me in the development of this book's message.

Sealy Yates, my literary agent and friend for more than twenty years, who always provides sound advice and "outside the lines" creativity.

Carrilyn Baker, my faithful associate for nearly two decades, who helped keep track of the numerous drafts of this book while juggling a multitude of other tasks at the same time—and always with excellence.

Ben Lovvorn, Nate Curtis, Patrick Heatherington, Vickie Sterling, and the entire Pathway to Victory team, who share the message of this book to millions of people throughout the world.

Amy Jeffress, my junior-high girlfriend and wife of forty years, who makes everything I am able to do possible.

1

What Difference Does a Future Heaven Make in My Life Today?

Keep seeking the things above, where Christ is, seated at the right hand of God. Set your mind on the things above, not on the things that are on earth.

Colossians 3:1–2

My ministry necessitates a lot of travel. Even now, as I'm beginning this book on heaven, I'm preparing for an international flight. Every time I journey to a distant destination, I make a mental checklist of things I need to accomplish before leaving and items I need to take with me on my trip. This is especially true if I know I'll be gone for an extended period of time.

Right now, I'm preparing for a trip to London. So the items on my to-do list are a bit more involved than if I were flying to New York for a day or two. For example, I need to contact the post office and the newspaper to have my deliveries stopped. I need to contact my credit card company and notify them of where I'll be so they don't think my card or identity has been stolen and freeze my account. I need to call the cell phone company to have my phone enabled for international service. I also need to check the exchange rate of dollars to pounds, see what the weather is going to be like so I can pack appropriately, and most important of all . . . make sure I have my ticket and passport. Without a ticket I can't board the plane; without a passport I can't enter the country.

Wise travelers go through a routine to prepare for leaving home—even if it's just for a weekend getaway. Yet very few people ever take time to prepare for the ultimate journey to a distant land everyone will take. My trip to London will only be for a couple of weeks, but the journey I'm referring to is a one-way trip that will last for eternity: it's the journey every Christian will embark upon to that "place called heaven."

Admittedly, many Christians do not consciously spend a lot of time thinking about heaven—perhaps you haven't either. That's understandable. The overwhelming responsibilities of living in this world eclipse much thought about living in the next world. Additionally, the fact that we know so little about our home in heaven makes it seem both remote and irrelevant to our existence.

Yet we all inwardly yearn for a better world—especially when we experience the unexpected bad report from the doctor, the betrayal of a friend, the breakup of an intimate relationship, or the death of a loved one. At those times we want to believe—we have to believe—that there is a better place in which to live. Gifted author Philip Yancey captures that reality when he writes:

> The Bible never belittles human disappointment . . . but it does add one key word: temporary. What we feel now, we will not always feel. Our disappointment is itself a sign, an aching, a hunger for something better. And faith is, in the end, a kind of homesickness—for a home we have never visited but have never once stopped longing for.[1]

This book is about that future home . . . heaven. Heaven is not some fanciful, imaginary destination created by well-intentioned individuals to keep you from being overwhelmed and crushed by the harsh realities of life. Jesus Christ—the One whom Christians are banking on for their eternal destiny—assures us that heaven is a real place:

> In My Father's house are many dwelling places; if it were not so, I would have told you; for I go to prepare a place for you. If I go and prepare a place for you, I will come again and receive you to Myself, that where I am, there you may be also. (John 14:2–3)

As we will see in the pages ahead, Jesus is in heaven right now overseeing the greatest construction project in history—our heavenly home. And if He goes to the trouble of creating such an elaborate home for us, we can be sure He will return to gather us up and escort us into that indescribable new destination He is preparing for us.

There are many reasons we should be thinking more about our future home in that "place called heaven," but the most obvious reason is this: our departure for our future home is both certain and relatively soon.

The Inevitability of Death

"The statistics on death are very impressive," one keen observer noted. "One out of every one dies."[2] And when death comes, it comes suddenly—and often unexpectedly.

"Man does not know his time," Solomon wrote. "Like fish caught in a treacherous net and birds trapped in a snare, so the sons of men are ensnared at an evil time when it suddenly falls on them" (Eccles. 9:12). The Old Testament patriarch Isaac didn't know the time of his passing. In the twilight of his life, he confessed, "I am old and I do not know the day of my death" (Gen. 27:2).

Soldiers on the battlefield face the prospect of death daily. So do cancer patients who have been told their case is terminal. But have you come to grips with the fact that you are going to die—and that this event could be just around the corner? If it's true that God has ordained every day of your life—including the day of your death—every second that passes moves you closer to the grave. That's a great reason to start thinking seriously about your eternal home.

Jesus once told a story of a farmer content with the abundance of his possessions. Tearing down his old barns to build bigger barns to store his grain, the foolish farmer said to himself: "You have many goods laid up for many years to come; take your ease, eat, drink and be merry" (Luke 12:19). But God had other plans: "You fool! This very night your soul is required of you" (v. 20). The word translated "required" refers to a loan that has come due. Our lives are simply on loan from God. He can "call in" the loan anytime He chooses!

Yet few of us—unless we're of advanced age or suffering with a terminal illness—actually live in light of death. We view death as a distant possibility. And heaven? Well, that's a subject for another time—or so we think.

But our departure from this life is certain. No one gets out of this world alive. "A person's days are determined," Job said. God "decreed the number of his months and . . . set limits he cannot exceed" (Job 14:5 NIV). Run all the miles you can and eat all the bran muffins you want; you're not going to live on earth one second longer than God has predetermined.

The realization that our time on earth is finite should certainly motivate us to use our time wisely. Moses prayed, "Teach us to number our days and recognize how few they are; help us to spend them as we should" (Ps. 90:12 TLB). Every time I read that verse I think about one of the godliest men I have ever known, Harold Warren. Years ago, Harold served as the chairman of the search committee that called me to become the pastor of First Baptist Church in Wichita Falls, Texas. In his office, Harold had a small blackboard filled with chalk marks. One day I asked him what those marks represented. "Each mark indicates how many days I have left until I reach my seventieth birthday," he said. "Every day I erase one to remind me how little time I have left and to encourage me to make the most of my remaining days." Harold lived a few years past his seventieth birthday. On the day after that milestone birthday, he began *adding* a mark, reminding himself that he was living on "borrowed time." Harold understood what it meant to "number our days."

Recognizing how limited our time on earth is should cause us to think about what awaits us in eternity. Christian author Joni Eareckson Tada, who became a quadriplegic in a diving accident in 1967, has thought a lot about heaven since that time: "Heaven may be as near as next year, or next week; so it makes good sense to spend some time here on earth thinking candid thoughts about that marvelous future reserved for us."[3]

In light of the certainty of heaven for Christians, Joni encourages believers to invest in relationships; to seek purity; to be honest; to give generously of time, talent, and treasure; and to share the gospel of Christ. Why? Because such choices carry eternal consequences and rewards, as we will see in future chapters.[4]

Perspectives from the Past

Joni Eareckson Tada isn't the only person who has thought about heaven. Writers, philosophers, and prophets throughout history have all given serious attention to what Shakespeare called "the undiscover'd country."[5] And most, if not all, have concluded that those who make the greatest impact on this life are those who think the most about the next life.

We've all heard the old cliché about being so heavenly minded that we're no earthly good. Some people use this idea to justify focusing their efforts and affections solely on this world—deluding themselves into thinking such a limited perspective is actually a virtue. Like the foolish farmer who acted as if he would live forever, these people fail to realize the brevity of this life and the length of eternity.

As C. S. Lewis observed, the problem with most Christians is not that they think about heaven *too much* but that they think about heaven *too little.*

> If you read history, you will find that the Christians who did most for the present world were precisely those who thought most of the next. The Apostles themselves, who set on foot the conversion of the Roman Empire, the great men who built up the Middle Ages, the English Evangelicals who abolished the Slave Trade, all left their mark on Earth, precisely because their minds were occupied with Heaven. It is since Christians have largely ceased to think of the other world that they have become so ineffective in this. Aim at Heaven and you will get Earth "thrown in": aim at Earth and you will get neither.[6]

Here is the great irony: the more we think about the next world, the more effective we become in this world. I've seen that principle illustrated in my life every time I've been in the process of transitioning to a new church. Whenever a new church has called me as its pastor, there has always been an intermediate time of about a month during which I'm wrapping up my work at my former church while at the same time thinking about my new church. Usually, those four weeks are the most productive of my entire tenure at the former church. Why? I know my time is limited, I'm motivated to leave my work in good shape, and I am free to make what I believe are the best decisions for the church—after all, they can't fire me since I'm already on the way out! What a liberating feeling.

The realization that we are headed to a new location called "heaven" should be great motivation for us to spend our limited time on earth productively. No need to be concerned about piling up a large amount of money—we'll leave it all behind when we depart. No reason to be fixated on what other people do to us or think about us—our calling to our new location is assured. Instead, grasping the reality of that "place called heaven" that awaits us should liberate us to invest our few remaining years on earth as wisely as possible.

As you review the lives of the men and women in the Old Testament who made the most profound impact on this world—such as Abel, Enoch, Noah, Abraham, Isaac, Jacob, and Sarah—you discover one common denominator: they were captivated by the hope of the next world.

> All these died in faith, without receiving the promises, but having seen them and having welcomed them from a distance, and having confessed that *they were strangers and exiles on the earth.* For those who say such things make it clear that *they are seeking a country of their own.* And indeed if they had been thinking of that country from which they went out, they would have had opportunity to return. But as it is, they desire a *better country*, that is, a *heavenly one.* Therefore God is not ashamed to be called their God; for *He has prepared a city for them.* (Heb. 11:13–16)

David also yearned for that "better country." In Psalm 42 he wrote:

> As the deer pants for the water brooks,
> So my soul pants for you, O God.
> My soul thirsts for God, for the living God;
> When shall I come and appear before God?
> (Ps. 42:1–2)

In the New Testament, Paul struggled with two desires: to depart for heaven as soon as possible and to remain on earth to fulfill his ministry.

> Knowing that while we are at home in the body we are absent from the Lord . . . [I] prefer rather to be absent from the body and to be at home with the Lord. (2 Cor. 5:6, 8)

Paul realized that every minute spent alive on earth was a minute away from the home Jesus had prepared for him in heaven. That's an interesting perspective of life few people consider. I'm thinking about that reality as I write these words. Shortly after I return from London, I will have to spend three days in Detroit, Michigan, fulfilling a speaking commitment. Now, I have nothing against Detroit, but Detroit isn't my home. I'd rather spend those three days in my comfortable and familiar home, enjoying my family. I was made for Dallas, not Detroit. Paul was made for heaven, not earth. He didn't want to spend one more minute here than absolutely necessary.

Yet Paul realized it was necessary to spend *some* time here on earth to fulfill the mission God had entrusted to him of guiding other people to heaven. To the Philippian Christians, Paul confessed:

> For to me, to live is Christ and to die is gain. . . . But I am hard-pressed from both directions, having the desire to depart and be with Christ, for that is very much better; yet to remain on in the flesh is more necessary for your sake. (Phil. 1:21, 23–24)

It wasn't just Paul who was torn between his duty in this world and his desire for the next world. Other early Christians also sensed the pull toward "a country of their own." Last year I visited the ancient catacombs underneath the city of Rome, which are painted with heavenly scenes of beautiful landscapes, children playing, and feasting. The tombs of Christian martyrs buried there bear heavenly minded inscriptions:

- "In Christ, Alexander is not dead, but lives—his body is resting in the grave."
- "He went to live with Christ."
- "He was taken up into his eternal home."[7]

Third-century church father Cyprian encouraged his congregation to "greet the day which assigns each of us to his own home, which snatches us hence, and sets us free from the snares of the world, and restores us to paradise and the [heavenly] kingdom." He then asked, "Who that has been placed in foreign lands would not hasten to return to his own country?" The answer was obvious: no one, because "we regard paradise as our country."[8]

But having their eyes set on that far country didn't mean these early believers were oblivious to what was taking place around them. In AD 125, an Athenian philosopher named Aristides wrote to the Roman Emperor Hadrian about the activities of Christians. After recounting a long list of their righteous acts benefiting believers and nonbelievers alike, Aristides told the emperor: "If any righteous person of their number passes away from the world they rejoice and give thanks to God, and they follow his body, as if he were moving from one place to another."[9]

A Glimpse of Heaven

For the follower of Jesus Christ, death *is* "moving from one place to another"—like moving from the frozen tundra of the arctic circle to the sun-kissed beaches of Hawaii. Paul described a Christian's change of location at death: being "absent from the body" means being "at home with the Lord" (2 Cor. 5:8).

If heaven is our future forever home, why wouldn't we want to know all we could about it? Imagine your employer tells you that you are going to be permanently transferred to a city you have never visited before: San Diego, California. You've seen a few pictures of San Diego and remember you had a cousin who used to live there, but for the most part you know nothing about the city. Don't you imagine you would try to discover the options for housing, the best schools for your children, something about the cost of living, the climate, and a hundred other things about your new location? Only a fool would say, "I'm too busy with work and family responsibilities now to invest any effort in finding out about my future home." Theologian J. C. Ryle wrote that every Christian will one day experience a similar—but eternal—"transfer":

> You are leaving the land of your nativity, you are going to spend the rest of your life in a new hemisphere. It would be strange indeed if you did not desire information about your new abode. Now surely, if we hope to dwell forever in that "better country, even a heavenly one," we ought to seek all the knowledge we can get about it. Before we go to our eternal home we should try to become acquainted with it.[10]

However, as we begin to search the Scriptures for information about this "place called heaven," we soon discover that the Bible doesn't tell us everything we want to know about our future home. What the Bible reveals is true but it's not exhaustive. Instead, God has given us a pencil sketch or line drawing of our future home.

For example, the apostle Paul received a personal tour of heaven when he was "caught up to the third heaven . . . into Paradise" (2 Cor. 12:2, 4).[11] Yet, this man who wrote most of the New Testament never jotted down a pen stroke of what he heard or saw in heaven! Why? Because what he heard were "inexpressible words, which a man is not permitted to speak" (v. 4).

And though the apostle John was given the most extensive vision of the future any Christian has ever received—recorded in the Book of Revelation—there were some aspects that John was commanded to "seal up . . . and do not write them" (Rev. 10:4). So why doesn't God tell us everything there is to know about heaven?

First, God knows that our minds are incapable of fully comprehending the complete magnificence of heaven. For example, how could you ever adequately describe the beauty of a sunset to a blind person who has never seen anything? What words would you sign to a deaf person to capture the all-encompassing majesty of Beethoven's Fifth Symphony? Our minds are designed to comprehend the experiences of this world but are incapable of processing the realities of the next world.

Additionally, if we knew everything about heaven we would never be able to concentrate on our God-given responsibilities here on earth. I realize this sounds like a contradiction to my earlier claim that being more heavenly minded makes us more earthly good, but it's not. Let me explain.

Suppose a child sits down at the dinner table and his mother places in front of him a plate of lima beans, which he normally wouldn't mind eating. But then his mother places a bowl of vanilla ice cream smothered in chocolate syrup and whipped cream on the table. What do you think the child will want to eat? The same thing you'd want to eat—the sundae! However, if the boy sits there with his plate of lima beans and his mother *promises* him an ice cream sundae after he eats his vegetables, then he'll dive into his lima beans with gusto, knowing something better is yet to come!

If God told us *everything* about heaven, we'd find it difficult to focus on the very important assignments God has charged us with during our brief stay here on earth. That is why God has given us just enough information about heaven to whet our appetite for the "sundae" that is yet to come.

Echoes of Eternity

The fact that God gives us only a glimpse of heaven shouldn't discourage us from discovering everything we can about our future home. Life is about much more than the seventy or so years we spend here on earth. Don't misunderstand what I'm saying: your life here on earth is extremely important. The choices you make, the character you form, and the affections you develop now will impact your life on the other side of the grave, as we'll see in chapter 8. As the fictitious Roman general-turned-gladiator Maximus Decimus Meridius told his men, "What we do in life echoes in eternity."[12]

Nevertheless, our existence beyond death deserves our serious consideration. As the Roman philosopher Seneca put it, "This life is only a prelude to eternity."[13] C. S. Lewis wrote about this in the final book of his Narnia series, *The Last Battle*. The children are involved in a terrible train wreck and are immediately transported to Narnia. They fear they'll be sent back to earth, but Aslan assures them that they've finally come home.

> "There *was* a real railway accident," said Aslan softly. "Your father and mother and all of you are—as you used to call it in the Shadowlands—dead. The term is over: the holidays have begun. The dream is ended: this is the morning."
>
> And as He spoke, He no longer looked to them like a lion; but the things that began to happen after that were so great and beautiful that I cannot write them. And for us this is the end of all the stories, and we can most truly say that they all lived happily ever after. But for them it was only the beginning of the real story. All their life in this world and all their adventures in Narnia had only been the cover and the title page: now at last they were beginning Chapter One of the Great Story which no one on earth has read: which goes on forever: in which every chapter is better than the one before.[14]

Four Benefits of Being "Heavenly Minded"

Indeed, if our brief time on earth is only the "cover and title page" of our eternal existence, it only makes sense that we would want to know what comes after the title page. Beyond satisfying our natural curiosity about what awaits us beyond the grave, contemplating the next life can result in four tangible benefits in this life.

1. Focusing on Heaven Reminds Us of the Brevity of Our Earthly Life

Life is short. Eternity is long. To illustrate this reality, Randy Alcorn asks people to take a piece of white paper and place a dot in the center, then draw a line from the dot to the edge of the page. It would look something like this:

The dot represents our years on earth, while the line represents eternity. Right now all of us are living inside the dot. Yet very few Christians think beyond the dot to the line—to the eternity that awaits us. How foolish it is to live for the dot that is only a blip on the screen of our eternal existence.[15]

Yet the dot and the line *are* connected to one another. As brief as our existence in this life is, it's very much connected to our eternal existence. There is no break between the dot and the line. My friend Bruce Wilkinson says it brilliantly: "Everything you do today matters forever."[16]

One of my closest friends and I both lost our parents when we were in our late twenties and early thirties. That shared experience has caused us both to talk frequently about how brief our time on earth is. When we are at dinner with our wives and something in the conversation touches on that topic, our wives will roll their eyes and say, "Oh no, here we go again with the 'life is short' speech!"

However, as much as I miss my parents, I see their "early departure" (at least from my perspective) as a gift from God that continually reminds me of how brief my life is. Their deaths remind me that while I live *in* the dot, I should never live *for* the dot. I must live for the line with eternity in mind. And that is true for you as well.

The New Testament writer James said it this way: "You do not know what your life will be like tomorrow. You are just a vapor that appears for a little while and then vanishes away" (James 4:14). And the apostle Peter observed:

> All people are like grass,
>   and all their glory is like the flowers of the field;
> the grass withers and the flowers fall.
>   (1 Pet. 1:24 NIV)

As one preacher in the Deep South said, "Life is like grass: It is sown, it is grown, it is mown, it is blown, and then it is gow-ne!" David not only agreed with this observation but prayed God would continually remind him of how brief his earthly life really was. In a psalm that echoed Moses's petition for the Lord to "teach us to number our days" (Ps. 90:12), David asked:

> LORD, make me to know my end
> And what is the extent of my days;
> Let me know how transient I am.
> Behold, You have made my days as handbreadths,
> And my lifetime as nothing in Your sight;
> Surely every man at his best is a mere breath.
>   (39:4–5)

Focusing on the reality and truth of heaven as we are going to do in the pages ahead is one very practical way to continually remind ourselves how fleeting our time on earth really is.

2. Focusing on Heaven Prepares Us for the Certainty of Judgment

"Everybody Is Going to Heaven" may be a popular song but it's also a horrendous lie. God's Word reveals that everybody is *not* going to heaven. In fact, very few people are going to heaven if Jesus can be trusted on this subject. The Lord urged people to "enter through the narrow gate; for the gate is wide and the way is broad that leads to destruction, and there are many who enter through it. For the gate is small and the way is narrow that leads to life, and there are few who find it" (Matt. 7:13–14).

Tragically, the majority of humanity is on the wrong road that ultimately leads to the wrong destination. From the moment we're born into this world we are on that road (or "way") that is heading away from God. It's the "way" of rebellion against God. As the prophet Isaiah wrote,

> All of us like sheep have gone astray,
> Each of us has turned to his own way. (Isa. 53:6)

No one has to do anything to end up in hell when he or she dies. All a person needs to do is continue traveling in the same direction he or she has been traveling since birth.

By contrast, relatively few people find the road that leads to heaven. In fact, to find that "way" a person must do a spiritual U-turn—which is the meaning of the biblical term *repent*. Repent (*metanoea*) means "to change one's mind." A simple definition of repentance is "a change of mind that leads to a change of direction." Only when a person admits that he or she is on the wrong road can he or she discover

27

the right road. Jesus was clear that He is the only "Way" that leads to eternal life: "I am the way, and the truth, and the life; no one comes to the Father but through Me" (John 14:6).

Notice Jesus said that at the end of the road to hell and the road to heaven is a "gate"—one gate opening to eternal damnation and the other gate opening to eternal salvation. In each case, the gate is called "judgment." The writer to the Hebrews declares a succinct but sobering truth: "It is appointed for men to die once and after this comes judgment" (Heb. 9:27).

There is simply no escaping the fact that each one of us—Christians and non-Christians alike—will face God's judgment when we arrive at the end of our lives on earth.

The "gate" or judgment for non-Christians is often called "the great white throne judgment" and results in eternal death. (We'll look at this judgment further in chapter 9.) The apostle John provides a sobering description of this judgment of all unbelievers in Revelation 20:

> Then I saw a great white throne and Him who sat upon it, from whose presence earth and heaven fled away, and no place was found for them. And I saw the dead, the great and the small, standing before the throne, and books were opened; and another book was opened, which is the book of life; and the dead were judged from the things which were written in the books, according to their deeds. And the sea gave up the dead which were in it, and death and Hades gave up the dead which were in them; and they were judged, every one of them according to their deeds. Then death and Hades were thrown into the lake of fire. . . . And if anyone's name was

not found written in the book of life, he was thrown into the lake of fire. (vv. 11–15)

Contrary to what many believe, Christians are *not* exempt from God's judgment. At the end of every Christian's life is also a "gate" or judgment—but it's a different judgment than the one non-Christians will face. This judgment or evaluation is often referred to as "the judgment seat of Christ." Paul emphatically declared:

> For we must all appear before the judgment seat of Christ, so that each one may be recompensed for his deeds in the body, according to what he has done, whether good or bad. (2 Cor. 5:10)

This is not a judgment of condemnation leading to hell, like the great white throne judgment. Instead, this is an evaluation leading to commendation by God and rewards that will greatly impact the kind of heaven we'll experience. (We'll explore this in detail in chapter 8.)

Reflecting upon the reality of heaven reminds us of the reality of God's judgment at the end of our lives and serves as an incentive to make certain that we'll experience the judgment that results in God's rewards rather than His condemnation.

3. Focusing on Heaven Motivates Us to Live Pure Lives

Most of the television interviews I do for cable news are taped in the late afternoon or are live in the evening. That means I must concentrate on keeping my clothes clean throughout the day. I tuck a napkin into my shirt collar at lunch to prevent stains on my tie. I immediately use a wet towel to wipe off any dirt on my suit jacket. And right before the camera rolls, someone runs a lint remover over my garment. All of this attention is necessary because the bright lights and high-definition television equipment are unforgiving and will reveal to millions of people any imperfections in my attire.

Similarly, there's a day coming when every Christian's "clothing" or actions will be placed under the glare of God's judgment and will reveal any imperfections. That "day" is the day of Christ's return in which "each man's work will become evident; for the day will show it" (1 Cor. 3:13). As we'll see in chapter 8, the purpose of this judgment is to determine not the believer's eternal destiny but his or her eternal rewards.

The Bible often uses clothing as a metaphor for our spiritual lives. It's helpful to understand that in biblical times people often wore two different types of tunics: an inner tunic (comparable to today's undergarments) that no one saw and an outer tunic that was visible to everyone.

Every Christian also wears two kinds of spiritual garments. Our "inner tunic" is our *judicial* righteousness—meaning our "right standing" with God—that God places on us when we trust in Christ as our Savior. Paul referred to our judicial righteousness when he prayed that on the day he finally met God he might "be found in Him, not having a righteousness of [his] own derived from the Law, but that which is through faith in Christ" (Phil. 3:9). Our "inner garment" of God's forgiveness is something we receive from Him. There is nothing we can do to improve it, soil it, or remove it.

But no one wants to walk around wearing only undergarments! That's why, to be properly dressed, we must put on our "outer tunic." This "outer tunic" represents a Christian's *ethical* righteousness, which is how we live after we become a Christian. While judicial righteousness refers to our "right standing" before God, ethical righteousness represents our "right acting" before God after we are saved.

The Bible compares a Christian's behavior after he or she is saved to these outer garments. Unlike the "one-size-fits-all" inner garment, there are a variety of external garments we can put on, ranging from stylish to hideous and clean to filthy. The apostle John encourages believers to be dressed in our best "clothes" when Christ returns. "It was given to [the church]," John wrote, "to clothe herself in fine linen, bright and clean; for the fine linen is the righteous acts of the saints" (Rev. 19:8).

You would never think of attending an elaborate, formal wedding in Bermuda shorts or a halter top. You would put on your finest tuxedo or dress for such a special occasion. However, even if you were wearing expensive clothes, no one would notice your finery if your garment had a humongous chocolate syrup stain on the front!

As Christians we should adorn our lives with the finest "garments" or good works we can—not to earn Christ's forgiveness but to receive His rewards when He returns and consummates the "marriage" between Himself and His church. We should be careful to keep our lives "clean" and not stain those righteous acts with sin.

Of course, that's easier said than done. We live in a sinful world in which pollution seeps from our culture like toxic waste bubbling up from a garbage heap. Being surrounded on every side with messages and images of immorality, rebellion, and lawlessness makes it hard to keep our character clean—to keep it from becoming saturated with the stench of sin. And it's getting more difficult as the days go by.

One of the best detergents for keeping our lives spotless is keeping our eyes focused on the promise of heaven. The writer to the Hebrews said that Moses, the son of royal privilege who was surrounded by the luxuries of Egypt, willingly endured "ill-treatment with the people of God" rather than enjoying "the passing pleasures of sin," because "he was looking to the reward" he would receive in heaven (Heb. 11:25–27).

Moses understood that the pleasures and the treasures of this world last only for a moment. In due time they will be consumed, along with all creation—just as Peter said.

> But the day of the Lord will come like a thief, in which the heavens will pass away with a roar and the elements will be destroyed with intense heat, and the earth and its works will be burned up. (2 Pet. 3:10, 12)

Peter then asked, "Since all these things are to be destroyed in this way, what sort of people ought you to be" (v. 11)? The answer is simple: we ought to be people of "holy conduct and godliness" (v. 11). Randy Alcorn illustrates why focusing on heaven can be a strong motivation for pursuing purity in this life:

> If my wedding date is on the calendar, and I'm thinking of the person I'm going to marry, I shouldn't be an easy target for seduction. Likewise, when I've meditated on Heaven, sin is terribly unappealing. It's when my mind drifts from Heaven that sin seems attractive. Thinking of Heaven leads

inevitably to pursuing holiness. Our high tolerance for sin testifies of our failure to prepare for Heaven.[17]

4. Focusing on Heaven Places Suffering in Perspective

One of the questions I'm asked most frequently as a pastor is "Why did God allow _____ (some horrific experience in their life) to happen?" God never completely answers the "why" question when it comes to suffering. However, He has given us the promise of heaven to put suffering in perspective. The apostle Paul—who was well acquainted with suffering—wrote confidently:

> For momentary, light affliction is producing for us an eternal weight of glory far beyond all comparison, while we look not at the things which are seen, but at the things which are not seen; for the things which are seen are temporal, but the things which are not seen are eternal. (2 Cor. 4:17–18)

Even though Paul had been shipwrecked, imprisoned, and beaten within an inch of his life on five different occasions, he described those horrific experiences as "momentary" and "light." How could Paul say such a thing? Was the apostle suffering from amnesia? No; his suffering could only be considered "momentary" and "light" when compared to the "eternal weight" of the future God had planned for him.

For example, you may be experiencing a difficulty you think will never end. Yet when compared to the length of eternity it is only "momentary." How long is eternity? One writer imagines a bird that comes once every million years to sharpen its beak on the top of Mount Everest. By the time the bird has succeeded in wearing that mighty mountain down to nothing—eternity will not have even begun! The time of our suffering on earth is "momentary" when compared to the eternality of our home in heaven!

Our afflictions—however unbearable they may seem—are also "light" when compared to the "weight" of heaven. Think of it this way: would you describe a two-thousand-pound block of concrete as "light" or "heavy"? Compared to a feather, it certainly is heavy. But compared to a fully fueled 777 jetliner, that concrete block is light.

Similarly, the most horrendous difficulties you experience in this life are light when compared to the indescribable future God is preparing for you in that place called heaven. Teresa of Avila observed, "In light of heaven, the worst suffering on earth, a life full of the most atrocious tortures on earth, will be seen to be no more serious than one night in an inconvenient hotel."[18] Focusing on the hope of heaven doesn't eliminate suffering in this world but it does help us put our suffering in perspective.

Heaven is the promise that God will eventually make all things right and that He will one day fulfill our deepest longings. Although God's promise is yet future, it should make a tremendous difference in our lives today. As Alcorn explained, "If we grasp it, [heaven] will shift our center of gravity and radically change our perspective on life."[19] This is the hope of heaven—that *all* of creation will receive what it has long desired: freedom from the crushing oppression of sin.

> For the anxious longing of the creation *waits eagerly* for the revealing of the sons of God. For the creation was subjected to futility, not willingly, but because of Him who subjected it, in hope that the creation itself also will be set free from

its slavery to corruption into the freedom of the glory of the children of God. For we know that the whole creation groans and suffers the pains of childbirth together until now. And not only this, but also we ourselves, having the first fruits of the Spirit, even we ourselves groan within ourselves, *waiting eagerly* for our adoption as sons, the redemption of our body. For in hope we have been saved, but hope that is seen is not hope; for who hopes for what he already sees? But if we hope for what we do not see, with perseverance *we wait eagerly for it*. (Rom. 8:19–25)

How we wait for this "place called heaven"—whether with anticipation or anxiety, whether with focused or unfocused living—matters both now and in the future. For what we do on earth today reverberates in the halls of heaven forever.

2

Is Heaven a Real Place
or Is It a State of Mind?

In My Father's house are many dwelling places; if it were not
so, I would have told you; for I go to prepare a place for you.

John 14:2

One morning in early 1971, famed Beatle John Lennon sat
down at his Steinway piano and composed what would become one of his greatest hits and an anthem of the age:
"Imagine." In a tribute to one-world utopian ideals, Lennon
asked us to imagine that neither heaven nor hell exists.

As one who dabbled in Hinduism but lived as a practical
atheist, it wasn't difficult for John Lennon to imagine no heaven
above us. From Hinduism, Lennon learned that god is everything and everything is god, and that heaven is everywhere and
nowhere at the same time. Therefore, the only hope at death is
breaking the cycle of reincarnation—the great "do over"—and
becoming absorbed into the "oneness" of the universal mind.

From atheism, Lennon learned that God is nothing and no one is God, and that heaven is nowhere because it doesn't exist—above us is only sky. Perhaps this stark conclusion is what led Lennon to imagine there's no hell—below us is only earth. After all, imagining no hell is the only hope atheists have.

Of course none of Lennon's musings about heaven answer the question of whether heaven is real or is merely a mental projection—a state of mind—of those who need the idea of heaven as a crutch for the harsh realities of life. Imagining heaven isn't real doesn't make heaven *un*real any more than imagining you're a turnip makes you a vegetable. Truth is not the sum of our imagination. Just because skeptics imagine heaven doesn't exist doesn't make it so.

Of course atheists quickly point out that just because we *can* imagine heaven doesn't make it real either. True enough. But atheists have long assumed that Christians have merely *imagined* heaven's reality and have accused people of faith of living in a fantasyland—of looking forward to a heaven that isn't there. "If it can't be proven scientifically that heaven exists, then it must not exist," they argue.

But, as my friend David Jeremiah counters, "Heaven is no figment of the imagination; nor is it a feeling, a state of mind, or the invention of man. Heaven is a literal place prepared by Christ for a prepared people."[1] And that's the truth we are going to explore in this chapter: the reality of heaven.

Heaven Is Real

If we accept the most basic definition of heaven, that it is "the abode of the Deity [of God],"[2] then we can assume God is the one true expert on the subject. Therefore, if we want to know whether heaven is real or simply a state of mind, we should turn to God's book, the Bible, to answer that question.

The most definitive answer to the question about the reality of heaven is found in John 14. But before we get there, understanding its background is important.

Four days had passed since Jesus's triumphal entry into Jerusalem. In the waning hours of His earthly life, Jesus sat down with His disciples for a final Passover meal. At some point during the meal, Jesus rose and wrapped a towel around His waist and began washing the disciples' feet. With this task complete, He announced: "one of you will betray me" (John 13:21 NLT). Then He said:

> Dear children, I will be with you only a little longer . . . but you can't come where I am going. So now I am giving you a new commandment: Love each other. Just as I have loved you, you should love each other. (vv. 33–34 NLT)

It was a troubling evening. Jesus was troubled because of what lay ahead of Him—the betrayal of Judas, the soul-wrenching prayer in the garden, the arrest, beatings, trials, and crucifixion. The disciples were troubled because they didn't know what the future held, especially in light of Jesus's increasingly frequent talk about His impending death.

The disciples' hearts pounded in their chests and questions throbbed in their minds: *Will Jesus's death signal the end of the movement we have been part of for the last three years? Will we ever see Him again? Will our leader's death result in our deaths as well?* None of it made sense; it was all very unsettling.

But Jesus reassured them with some of the most familiar words the Lord ever spoke. Though they couldn't immediately accompany Him on His journey back to His Father, in due time Jesus would return and take them to heaven—to the "Father's house."

> Do not let your heart be troubled; believe in God, believe also in Me. In My Father's house are many dwelling places; if it were not so, I would have told you; for I go to prepare a place for you. If I go and prepare a place for you, I will come again and receive you to Myself, that where I am, there you may be also. (John 14:1–3)

When Jesus told the disciples about the "Father's house," He didn't speak of a place that "exists" in the fantasyland of our minds. Jesus used language that describes a real location. "Place" (*topos*) is used three times in John 14:2–3. This Greek word serves as the root for our word *topography*—the act of detailing the actual, physical features of land on a map. When used in the New Testament, *topos* almost always indicates a locatable and inhabited space. In some contexts it refers to a city or region;[3] in others it refers to an individual residence—a house or a room, which is the case in John 14:2–3.

But it's more than just the word *topos* that tells us heaven is real. Jesus also said "In My Father's house are many *dwelling* places" (v. 2). The Greek word for "dwelling" is *mone* and can also be translated as "habitat," "lodging," or "domicile."[4] Each of these words describes something that is real and physical.

When Amy and I started our family and our two daughters came along, we had a nursery for them. But when they were old enough, each of the girls had her own room—a place for them to paint and decorate as they chose and to play in and study in (more play than study!). They each had a real, physical place in our home to call their own. That's what Jesus is preparing for each one of us—a physical place for us to live in for eternity. And it's a place so fabulous that it defies imagination.

If Jesus's use of "place" and "dwelling" isn't enough to prove the reality of heaven, He twice said, "I *go and prepare* a place for you" (vv. 2–3). The act of going and preparing speaks to something tangible, not intangible. Jesus's "going" refers to His death, resurrection, and ascension. After giving final instructions to His disciples, the Bible records:

> [Jesus] was lifted up while [the disciples] were looking on, and a cloud received Him out of their sight. And as they were gazing intently into the sky while He was going, behold, two men in white clothing stood beside them. They also said, "Men of Galilee, why do you stand looking into the sky? This Jesus, who has been taken up from you into heaven, will come in just the same way as you have watched Him go into heaven." (Acts 1:9–11)

The ascension of Jesus occurred on the Mount of Olives, outside the walls of Jerusalem—a physical, geographical location where I've stood many times. So when Jesus ascended from this real place (the Mount of Olives), where did He go? It's nonsensical to say Jesus left the physical earth and ascended into some metaphysical state of mind. Jesus traveled from one geographical location (the Mount of Olives) to another geographical location (heaven). And it is in heaven that Jesus is preparing a place for us. When the time is right, Jesus promised, "I will come again and receive you to Myself, that where I am, there you may be also" (John 14:3).

Where Is This "Place Called Heaven"?

Throughout His earthly ministry, Jesus made it clear that the path to heaven was paved by belief in Him—in His death and resurrection. After all the time they had spent with Jesus, the disciples should have known that, which is why Jesus told them, "you know the way where I am going" (v. 4). But they didn't know. They didn't fully understand that the "Father's house" was heaven (the where) and that going there required faith in Christ (the Way). So Thomas asked, "Lord, we do not know where You are going, how do we know the way?" (v. 5). In other words, if we don't know the destination, we can't know the direction.

To help them recalibrate their spiritual GPS, Jesus said to His disciples, "I am the way, and the truth, and the life; no one comes to the Father but through Me" (v. 6). The only way to heaven is through faith in Christ.[5] But where exactly is heaven? Jesus doesn't tell us, but the Bible may offer us one clue.

Scripture seems to indicate that heaven is "up." How do we know that? While Satan is not usually a reliable source of information for much of anything, his words occasionally reflect truth. Remember that Satan was originally God's highest-ranking angel, named Lucifer. But, discontent with his rank as God's second in command, Lucifer decided to mount a rebellion against God's authority, attempting to grab the title of "Sovereign Ruler" for himself. Lucifer's war cry against God included the words:

> I will *ascend* to heaven;
> I will *raise* my throne *above the stars* of God.
>   (Isa. 14:13)

"Ascend," "raise," and "above the stars" all indicate that the direction of heaven is upward. As we've already seen in Acts 1:9–11, Jesus's departure from earth into heaven was upward into the sky. Luke—the author of Acts—wrote that Jesus was "lifted up" into the clouds (1:9), and that the disciples were watching Him, "gazing intently into the sky" (v. 10). When the two angels addressed the disciples, they asked: "Why do you stand looking into the sky?" And then the angels said: "This Jesus, who has been taken *up* from you into heaven, will come in just the same way as you have watched Him go into heaven," meaning that He will come *down* from heaven at His second coming (v. 11).

Both God's holy angels and Lucifer indicate that the location of heaven is upward. Also, consider Paul's description of Jesus as the One "who descended" in His humanity as also being the One "who ascended far above all the heavens" (Eph. 4:10). Above us is more than sky. Above us is God's dwelling place.

But when people wonder about the location of heaven, they are usually thinking about more than the direction it is in. They are really inquiring about the realm in which heaven exists. They want to know if heaven is part of our time-space universe—far, far away, perhaps, but still somewhere that can be located. Or does heaven exist in a completely different dimension, outside of and beyond time and space (like the "fifth dimension beyond that which is known to man" described in the classic TV series *The Twilight Zone*)?

To answer that question, we need to distinguish between the present heaven where God resides and the future heaven Jesus is constructing for us. The present heaven—sometimes called by theologians the "intermediate state"—is where Christians go immediately when they die to enjoy the presence of the Lord as Paul describes: "We are of good courage, I say, and prefer rather to be absent from the body and to be at home with the Lord" (2 Cor. 5:8).

The future heaven is where all believers will one day spend eternity, and this future heaven is still under construction. It is the "place" Jesus is preparing for us now—and its final location may surprise you, as we will see in the next section.

The idea of a present heaven and a future heaven is sometimes confusing. But think of it like this: couples who plan to retire sometimes buy a little plot of land next to a lake, or in the mountains, or along the seashore and begin to build a house on it. They may continue to live in their existing home or move to an apartment while their future retirement home is under construction. Their current address may be wonderful—plush and comfortable—but it's only temporary. The couple could truly be said to be in an "intermediate state" as they await the completion of their future home. In the same way, those who are in heaven today (the present heaven) are enjoying a wonderful existence in the presence of God while waiting for the completion of their final, forever home (the future heaven).

Since this truth about both a present heaven and future heaven is a surprise to many Christians, let's look more closely at the difference between the two.

The Present Heaven

Theologians often point out that the Bible refers to three heavens. The first heaven is earth's atmosphere. It contains the air we breathe and the space in which birds and jetliners fly. The second heaven is what we often refer to as "outer space," where we find the planets, stars, and billions of galaxies that populate this vast universe.

The third heaven represents the presence of God. This is where all Christians immediately go when they die. (We will discuss this in detail in chapter 4.) It is sometimes called Paradise—the place where Jesus assured the thief on the cross he would go the moment he died. At some point in his life, Paul was caught up into this third heaven, where he heard "inexpressible words" (2 Cor. 12:4). When most Christians speak of heaven this is the heaven they mean—the one that is "up." This is the "present heaven" I referred to in the last section.

The Future Heaven

But there is also a fourth heaven—a future "heaven" God is preparing for us right now. This is the place of our future and forever home—and it is a geographical location. This fourth heaven includes the "new heaven" and "new earth" and the "new Jerusalem" John described in Revelation 21–22 as coming down from the third heaven to the newly created earth. The fourth heaven will literally be "heaven on earth." This future heaven will be the place where all believers—Old Testament saints, New Testament saints, and all Christians from the time of Jesus's death and resurrection to date—will live for eternity.

At some future point the present heaven—where God, the angels, and all believers who have died are—will be combined with the future heaven—the new heaven, new earth, and New Jerusalem. This will not take place until after the rapture, the seven-year tribulation, the battle of Armageddon, the millennial kingdom, and the great white throne judgment—just as Scripture states.[6]

The apostle John recorded in his end-times vision that he "saw a new heaven and a new earth; for the first heaven and the first earth passed away. . . . And I saw the holy city, new Jerusalem, coming down out of heaven from God, made ready as a bride adorned for her husband" (Rev. 21:1–2).

What will this new heaven and new earth and New Jerusalem be like? Before answering that question we must first understand the nature of "newness."

What Does "New" Really Mean?

What did John mean when he wrote that he saw "a *new* heaven and a *new* earth; for the first heaven and the first earth passed away" (v. 1)? Does this mean God will replace the first and second heavens (earth's atmosphere and outer space) and the earth we know with a re-created (new) heaven and earth? This certainly seems to be the case, at least according to the apostle Peter:

> By His word the present heavens and earth are being reserved for fire, kept for the day of judgment and destruction of ungodly men. . . . But the day of the Lord will come like a thief, in which the heavens will pass away with a roar and the elements will be destroyed with intense heat, and the earth and its works will be burned up. Since all these things

are to be destroyed in this way, what sort of people ought you to be in holy conduct and godliness, looking for and hastening the coming of the day of God, because of which the heavens will be destroyed by burning, and the elements will melt with intense heat! But according to His promise we are looking for new heavens and a new earth, in which righteousness dwells. (2 Pet. 3:7, 10–13)[7]

John (in Rev. 21) and Peter (in 2 Pet. 3) both used the same Greek root word for "pass away"—*parerchomai*. But Peter further describes what it means for the earth and the solar systems, along with their most basic building blocks ("the elements"), to "pass away." They "will be destroyed with intense heat . . . burned up" (v. 10). And just in case he wasn't clear the first time, Peter repeats: "the heavens will be destroyed by burning, and the elements will melt with intense heat!" (v. 12). John most likely meant the same thing when he wrote in Revelation 21:1, "the first heaven and the first earth passed away."

Scripture is silent on exactly how God will burn up the universe, but theologians and scientists have speculated about the intensity of heat required to destroy the earth. Some believe a nuclear holocaust, along the lines of Nagasaki and Hiroshima, only unimaginably more powerful, could incinerate the universe. Nuclear explosions produce heat of tens of millions of degrees, which would certainly explain how "the elements will melt with intense heat."

Others believe a massive asteroid fifty or sixty miles wide hitting the earth could be the catalyst for the destruction of the planet—perhaps like John's description of one of the judgments at the end of the tribulation: "And huge hailstones, about one hundred pounds each, came down from heaven upon men" (Rev. 16:21).

But all of this is just guesswork, something fun for scientists to speculate about. The truth is we don't know how God will destroy the heavens and the earth. But since He spoke the universe into being with just a word, it would be no problem for Him to destroy it with just a word.

But why does God need to destroy the old heavens and old earth to create a new heaven and a new earth? God created the existing heavens and earth as recorded in Genesis 1 and pronounced them "good." But sin spoiled all of that. Like leaving a classic 1955 Corvette to rot in the elements until it becomes a rust bucket, sin so corrupted our physical environment that God wants to create a better, newer model—one in which perfect righteousness dwells.

In some of the wealthier areas in my city, Dallas, it's not uncommon for wealthy individuals to buy old homes and completely raze them and their foundations, leaving only dirt. These homes aren't rickety haunted houses. In fact, most of the time they are beautiful old structures with intricate woodwork, stained glass windows, and detailed craftsmanship. So why demolish a perfectly good (old) house? Because the owners want something bigger and newer.

God is going to do something similar with the old heavens and earth. And when this happens—after the great white throne judgment and before believers enter into the New Jerusalem—God will have fulfilled His promise in Isaiah 65:17: "For behold, I create new heavens and a new earth; And the former things will not be remembered or come to mind."

The "New Earth" Versus the Present Earth

Ultimately, we won't go up to heaven and leave this earth behind forever. Instead, God will bring the new heaven down to a newly created earth. In many ways this new earth will resemble our present earth—but it will also be vastly improved.

This new earth—like the old one—will be *physical* in nature (Rev. 21). Resurrected believers with new bodies—bodies like Jesus after His resurrection—require a physical home. Disembodied spirits might be able to live in some ethereal, spiritual dimension, but physical human beings need an earthy, physical dimension. And God will create such a place for us—a physical place for physically transformed bodies.

The new earth will be not only physical in nature but also *familiar*. Frankly, many Christians aren't that anxious about the prospect of going to heaven because they believe heaven will be completely different from anything they've experienced before. We tend to be creatures of habit—I certainly am—and it's hard to get excited about something that's unfamiliar to us. Heaven—the new earth—won't be like moving from your hometown to a city in a foreign country where you don't know the streets or neighborhoods.

As I used to hear my longtime pastor and predecessor Dr. W. A. Criswell say, "I wouldn't look forward to God sending me to live for eternity on some planet I know nothing about a hundred million miles away. I like almost everything about earth. The only things I don't like are the tears, the separation, and the heartache. But those will be gone forever in heaven."

Indeed they will! In John's experience, he heard a voice saying, "[God] will wipe away every tear from their eyes;

and there will no longer be any death; there will no longer be any mourning, or crying, or pain; the first things have passed away" (Rev. 21:4). The curse leveled against this present world (described in Gen. 3) will be lifted and all of redeemed humankind will enjoy the world as God originally created it. Those who live on the new earth will experience unbroken fellowship with God and one another in joyous, loving relationships untainted by sin.

One of the most dramatic changes in the new earth will be the absence of the oceans. When John saw his vision of the new heaven and new earth, he said there would be "no longer any sea" (Rev. 21:1). We know the capital city of the new earth, the New Jerusalem, will gush with fresh, life-giving water (22:1), but it's not exactly clear why the new earth will have no oceans. Some speculate that the absence of the seas in the new earth is to provide more inhabitable space for citizens of heaven, since the oceans make up three-fourths of our current planet's surface.[8] Others say that because the seas are made up of salt, which is a preservative, they are unnecessary because there will be no decay in the new earth.[9]

At times I wonder if I will miss the salty air on my face and the sand between my toes—the beach vacation I enjoy every year. But I'm confident that for whatever reason God has for not re-creating the oceans, my first day on the new earth will make all my combined vacations on the old earth seem like an extended stay in a poorly maintained budget motel!

It's not just the oceans that will be missing from the new world. The new heavens will have no sun or moon. John wrote: "And the city [the New Jerusalem] has no need of the sun or of the moon to shine on it" (21:23).

Heaven has no need of these light sources because Jesus, the Light of the World, will illuminate the New Jerusalem for eternity. The new heaven and new earth will exist in perpetual daytime—"there will be no night there" (Rev. 21:25; 22:5)—fulfilling Isaiah's prophecy:

> No longer will you have the sun for light by day,
> Nor for brightness will the moon give you light;
> But you will have the LORD for an everlasting light,
> And your God for your glory. (Isa. 60:19)

Because the glory of Christ will shine forth, heaven will be a place of absolute safety—which we will discuss further in the next section.

Not only will oceans and darkness be missing from the new earth but so will preachers like myself! Preachers have two primary responsibilities: to proclaim the gospel and to condemn sin. But since "the earth will be filled with the knowledge of the glory of the LORD" (Hab. 2:14) and "there will no longer be any curse" (Rev. 22:3), I'll be looking for new work. A universal love for and devotion to God will permeate the new earth, meaning that we will no longer feel the sting of sin experienced every day in this world. Rather, our lives will be filled with uninterrupted and unending joy.

The New Earth's Capital: New Jerusalem

When Jesus told His disciples He was returning to His Father's house to prepare a place for them, the place He had in mind was a city that will be the focal point of the new earth: the New Jerusalem. This was the same city Abraham had long desired to find: "For he was looking for the city which has foundations, whose architect and builder is God" (Heb. 11:10).

The New Jerusalem—the "city of My God" (Rev. 3:12)—is an actual, physical city being built by Jesus in the present third heaven: the abode of God. I often say that the New Jerusalem is the ultimate in prefab housing! It's being built in one location but will be transported to another location. After the re-creation of the new heavens and new earth, the New Jerusalem will descend out of the third heaven and rest upon the re-created earth:

> And I saw the holy city, new Jerusalem, coming down out of heaven from God, made ready as a bride adorned for her husband. . . . And [the angel] carried me away in the Spirit to a great and high mountain, and showed me the holy city, Jerusalem, coming down out of heaven from God. (21:2, 10)

Though the New Jerusalem is a real city—complete with buildings, streets, and residences occupied by people who are involved in bustling activities, cultural events, and worship—it will be unlike any city we've ever seen.

Its *size* is overwhelming. For many, the gargantuan size of the New Jerusalem is its most striking feature. In Revelation 21:16 John describes an angel with a golden rod who measures the city's cube-shaped width, length, and height and finds it to be a staggering fifteen hundred miles![10] This makes the city's surface area two million square miles. By comparison, New York City is a puny 305 square miles.[11] With an area that large, if we placed New Jerusalem in the middle of the United States its borders would stretch from Canada to Mexico and from the Appalachian Mountains to California.

The height of the city is also mind-boggling. If the average story in a skyscraper is twelve feet high, the New Jerusalem will have 660,000 stories. By comparison, the tallest building in the world, Burj Khalifa in Dubai, is a puny 2,717 feet high, with 163 stories. One World Trade Center, which replaced the twin towers in New York City, is a mere 1,776 feet high, with 104 stories. And if this wasn't enough, the thickness of the walls in the heavenly city is "seventy-two yards" (Rev. 21:17)—nearly three-quarters of the length of an American football field!

Such an overwhelming measurement has led many to believe that the dimensions of the New Jerusalem are symbolic, not literal. But there's no logical reason to take these figures figuratively. In fact, John went out of his way to say that these dimensions were given in "human measurements" (v. 17).

When you think about it, a large, magnificent city made of precious stones, large pearls, and pure gold is one befitting our magnificent Creator. God has been known to create some fairly large objects—think Mount Everest, the Pacific Ocean, or the Milky Way galaxy. But more than that, God is also a God of beauty—consider a sunset over an ocean, a sunrise over a mountain, the tiny feet of a newborn baby, or a bride walking down the aisle. If God would bestow such beauty upon our fallen world, can you imagine what splendor He will lavish on the heavenly city He is preparing for us to live in for all eternity?

Additionally, the New Jerusalem must be large enough to accommodate the redeemed of all ages. We don't know how many residents will actually live in the New Jerusalem—only God knows that—but theologian Ron Rhodes wrote:

One mathematician calculated that if the New Jerusalem is shaped like a cube, it would have enough room for 20 billion residents if each individual residence were a massive 75 acres. There would also be plenty of room left over for parks and streets and other features that you'd likely see in any major city.[12]

The city itself is constructed of "a great and high wall, with twelve gates"—three facing north, three facing south, three facing east, and three facing west (Rev. 21:12–13). Each gate bears one of the names of the tribes of Israel. And stationed at each gate is an angel. The walls, the gates, and the angels—though very real—symbolize eternal *protection* from Satan, demons, and unbelievers.

Gates in ancient cities were always closed at night to protect the citizens sleeping inside. That practice continues today. Gated communities keep their entrances closed at night. Even "the happiest place on earth"—Disneyland—locks its gates every evening after the guests leave. But in the New Jerusalem the gates never close. They don't need to because Satan and his followers can never attack God's people or His city; they are eternally quarantined in the lake of fire.

In the daytime (for there will be no night there) its gates will never be closed . . . and nothing unclean, and no one who practices abomination and lying, shall ever come into it, but only those whose names are written in the Lamb's book of life. (vv. 25, 27)

My brother, who is a police officer, will also have to find another job because there won't be an HPD—Heavenly Police

Department. Heaven won't have prisons, courthouses, or lawyers. There will be no need to close the gates of heaven or even the doors of our new homes to keep evildoers away from us. There will be no evildoers residing in the new heaven and the new earth who need to be arrested, defended, or imprisoned.

That means in the New Jerusalem we will never have to lock our doors or hide our valuables. We can leave our windows open and the keys in our cars because it will be a place of perfect peace and protection.

Its *permanence* is eternal. The New Jerusalem will also be constructed to last forever, which seems to be the significance of the "twelve foundation stones" (Rev. 21:14). Each one is inscribed with the names of the twelve apostles.[13] Military brats, pastors' kids, and missionary kids can especially appreciate this. No more moving from one place to another; no more changing schools or making new friends; no more feelings of being uprooted, of not belonging, or of being the outsider. Heaven will not only be home, it will *feel* like home. It's a place where we can plant eternal roots.

Its *splendor* is incredible. The heavenly city is not just a place of peace, protection, and permanence; it's also a place of unimaginable beauty—even more spectacular than Oz's imaginary Emerald City. The New Jerusalem will be Paradise regained.

Because God dwells there, His glory will cause the city to shimmer like the luster of a diamond under the noonday sun—like "crystal-clear jasper," as John put it (v. 11). In the midst of the city sits God's throne, from which pours forth a life-giving and life-sustaining river—"clear as crystal," John wrote (22:1).

Coors advertises that their beer is brewed with "pure Rocky Mountain spring water" (as a Baptist pastor I cannot verify if that is true!). But in comparison to the water that gushes from God's throne, drinking Rocky Mountain spring water will be like drinking sludge. The "river of the water of life" (Rev. 22:1) will satisfy and bless all who drink deeply from its depths. And our thirst—both physical and spiritual—will be quenched forever.

Planted along the banks of this river is "the tree of life" (v. 2). After their sin, Adam and Eve were banished from the Garden of Eden and barred from the tree—Paradise lost. But in the New Jerusalem, access to the tree is free and unfettered—Paradise restored. The tree perpetually bears a different kind of fruit each month to sustain the immortality of the city's citizens. And the leaves of the tree give everlasting health to all the residents of the new earth:

> On either side of the river was the tree of life, bearing twelve kinds of fruit, yielding its fruit every month; and the leaves of the tree were for the healing of the nations. (v. 2)[14]

I don't pretend to understand what all of this means, but one thing is certain: on the new earth there will be no doctors to wait for, no hospital food to gag on, and no insurance companies to wrangle with because there will be no sickness.

One last thing: unlike the Old Jerusalem, in which the Temple was the central feature, the New Jerusalem will have "no temple" (21:22). Rather, the presence of God and of Jesus will turn the whole city into a temple. And it is there—in that very real "place called heaven"—that we'll live and play and work and worship God forever.

Heaven Is beyond Imagination

Jesus has gone to prepare a place for you. A place more beautiful than any place you've ever seen; a place of peace and protection; a place that will literally be Paradise on earth. And the place Jesus is preparing, He is preparing with you in mind. "Your place in heaven will seem to be made for you and you alone," C. S. Lewis wrote, "because you were made for it—made for it stitch by stitch as a glove is made for a hand."[15]

The popular Christian contemporary song says, "I can only imagine." The truth is the home Jesus is preparing for you is beyond imagination.

3

Have Some People
Already Visited Heaven?

It is appointed for men to die once and after this comes
judgment.

Hebrews 9:27

"God is calling me."

Those were the last words of the great nineteenth-century
American evangelist Dwight L. Moody. The famed preacher
had dedicated his life to the preaching and teaching of the
gospel. Like Billy Graham who followed him, Moody traveled the world sharing the good news of Christ's death and
resurrection, sometimes in revivals where thousands heard him
preach. And like Graham, Moody ministered to some of the
most politically powerful men of his day. But on December 22,
1899, Moody died in his East Northfield, Massachusetts, home.

The fact that Moody died is not noteworthy—that fate
awaits us all. What makes Moody's death interesting is that he

may have gained a glimpse of heaven before his actual death. According to the story published in the *New York Times*, Moody said, "I see earth receding; Heaven is opening; God is calling me."[1] Based on those who've had "near-death experiences"—or NDEs as they are often called—and those who study them, Moody's description of seeing earth fading, as if he were outside of his body and traveling through space, and heaven looming before him, is a classic near-death experience.

Raymond Moody, the father of the NDE craze and the great-nephew of the famous evangelist, believes his uncle did have a near-death experience, a term he coined in his 1975 bestseller, *Life After Life*. His seminars on near-death experiences and the popularity of his book fostered a movement that today includes the International Association for Near-Death Studies (IANDS), which is a research foundation that began in 1981, the *Journal of Near-Death Studies* (JNDS), and a glut of consumer-driven books and movies about NDEs. But there is one important difference between the near-death experiences Raymond Moody describes and the experience his uncle had: D. L. Moody never came back after death to tell people what he had seen in heaven.

With so much attention on the afterlife and so many stories in the media, what are we to make of near-death experiences? What does the Bible say about NDEs? And what can those who claim to have had a near-death experience tell us about heaven—if anything?

What Are Near-Death Experiences?

Before we can evaluate the validity of near-death experiences, we must first understand what they are. A good place to begin is with a definition. IANDS defines a near-death experience as "a profound psychological event that may occur to a person close to death or, if not near death, in a situation of physical or emotional crisis. Because it includes transcendental and mystical elements, an NDE is a powerful event of consciousness." They are quick to add, however, "it is not a mental illness."[2]

NDErs, as those who have had a near-death experience call themselves, typically share a common experience, following a similar order of events. The usual experience and sequence includes the following:

- Having the sensation of floating upward and viewing the scene around one's "dead" body.
- Traveling through a tunnel, or a dark space, toward a light.
- Spending time in a beautiful, otherworldly realm.
- Meeting God, Jesus, and/or angels.
- Encountering deceased loved ones, relatives, and friends.
- Seeing the story of one's life passing in review, as if watching a movie.
- Having the sensation of overwhelming peace and love—though some have reported experiencing terrifying scenes of demons and distress.
- Approaching a barrier of some sort, signaling the point of no return.
- Being called back and reluctantly agreeing to return to one's body and life.

Such an experience can be transformative. "It offers the possibility of an escape from something that holds you back, and a transformation into something better," Gideon Lichfield, a reporter who has studied NDEs, wrote. "If the NDE happened during a tragedy, it provides a way to make sense of that tragedy and rebuild your life. If your life has been a struggle with illness or doubt, an NDE sets you in a different direction: you nearly died, so something has to change."[3]

You may have never had a near-death experience, but chances are you've come close to death at some point in your life. Some illness or close call has brought your mortality into sharper focus. And that brush with death can be life-altering.

One of my associates told me of an incident he had while canoeing with family and friends when his canoe became wedged against a truck-sized boulder in the middle of the river. In a split second water poured into the canoe and forced it sideways. Knowing the canoe would capsize, he grabbed his six-year-old daughter just before being thrown into the turbulent waters. He could do nothing for his ten-year-old son, who, despite wearing a life vest, went under.

Finding his footing, my friend placed his daughter on top of the boulder and began a frantic search for his son. Fortunately, the boy popped up a few yards downriver and was pulled into another canoe. That evening, back in camp, my friend couldn't sleep. He spent the night in tearful prayer, thanking God for saving his children's lives. All concerns about work, debts, and mortgages—the stuff of life—instantly disappeared. It was as near to death as he had ever come (and as near to losing his children as he ever hopes to come) and it radically changed his life.

Coming face-to-face with the prospect of death—whether your own or that of someone you love—can be jolting. Such an experience is a stark reminder of the brevity of life . . . and the length of eternity. So it makes sense that those who have "died" and experienced the sensation of leaving their body and traveling to a world of peace and love would never be the same after they "return" to life on this side of the grave.

However, just because someone has had a life-changing experience like an NDE doesn't mean his or her experience is real. But valid or not, no one can deny that near-death experiences are becoming increasingly popular.

Why Are Stories about Near-Death Experiences So Popular?

Books about near-death experiences regularly top the best-seller lists because they supposedly allow us to pull back the curtain and discover the answer to the greatest mystery of all: What awaits us on the other side of the grave? Is there really an existence beyond death? If so, is that existence the same for everyone? And can those who claim to have had an NDE tell us anything about the reality of heaven or hell?

Don Piper's 2004 book, *90 Minutes in Heaven: A True Story of Death and Life*, created a resurgence of interest in NDEs. His book was followed by Bill Wiese's terrifying account of hell, published in 2006: *23 Minutes in Hell: One Man's Story about What He Saw, Heard, and Felt in That Place of Torment*. Since then, there have been an onslaught of NDE books, including Nancy Botsford's *A Day in Hell: Death to Life to Hope* (2010), Eben Alexander's *Proof of Heaven: A Neurosurgeon's Journey into the Afterlife* (2012), and Mary Neal's *To Heaven and Back: The True Story of a Doctor's Walk with God* (2012).

But none of these books has been more popular than Todd Burpo and Lynn Vincent's *Heaven Is for Real: A Little Boy's Astounding Story of His Trip to Heaven and Back* (2010). This megaselling book recounts the story of four-year-old Colton Burpo, who "died" during emergency surgery, came back to life, and told his family about his three-minute trip to heaven. While in heaven, Colton claims to have seen his sister, whom his mother miscarried (and about whom his parents had told him nothing), his great-grandfather (whom he had never met), John the Baptist, Jesus, God the Father (who has wings), and the Holy Spirit, who apparently is bluish in color and transparent. The book has sold over ten million copies and spent over two hundred weeks on the *New York Times* bestseller list.[4]

But not every book about near-death experiences has been so well received, and at least one of those books has been fabricated. *The Boy Who Came Back from Heaven: A True Story*, by Kevin and Alex Malarkey, tells the story of Alex, who "died" and went to heaven after an automobile accident in 2004. Alex suffered brain trauma and severe spinal and neck injuries, leaving him a quadriplegic.

Capitalizing on the popularity of NDE books, a leading Christian publisher put the book out in 2010. However, five years after the book's release, Alex wrote an open letter recanting the contents of the book, confessing that he had lied. He asked Christian booksellers to pull the books from shelves.

"Please forgive the brevity," his letter began, "but because of my limitations I have to keep this short. I did not die. I did not go to heaven. I said I went to heaven because I thought it would get me attention."[5] Days later, the publisher released a statement: "We are saddened to learn that Alex Malarkey, co-author of 'The Boy Who Came Back from Heaven' is now saying that he made up the story of dying and going to heaven. Given this information, we are taking the book out of print."[6]

The popularity of these NDE books goes beyond our natural curiosity about the unknown. Implanted deep inside each of us is a longing for this "place called heaven." While there is much to love about earth—its people and places—we instinctively know there must be something more, something better. King Solomon wrote that God has "set eternity in [our] heart" (Eccles. 3:11), meaning we possess a deep-seated desire and natural inquisitiveness about what awaits us on the other side of death.

But where are we to look for the answers about what really happens to us after we die? Read carefully the confession of Alex Malarkey:

> When I made the claims I did [in his book *The Boy Who Came Back from Heaven*], I had never read the Bible. People have profited from lies, and continue to. They should read the Bible, which is enough. The Bible is the only source of truth. Anything written by man cannot be infallible. It is only through repentance of your sins and a belief in Jesus as the Son of God, who died for your sins (even though he committed none of his own) . . . that you can be forgiven [and can] learn of heaven. . . . I want the whole world to know that the Bible is sufficient.[7]

God has provided us with a wealth of information about the future that awaits Christians and non-Christians after death. Although God hasn't told us everything we may *want* to know, He has revealed everything we *need* to know. As Malarkey confesses, "the Bible is sufficient."

The Bible is sufficient because the Bible is true. And when it comes to evaluating NDEs, we must test all claims against its teaching. To do so fulfills John's command to "not believe every spirit, but test the spirits to see whether they are from God" (1 John 4:1), and puts us in the category of the wise Bereans who examined the Scriptures carefully to see whether Paul's preaching was true (Acts 17:11).

So let's see what God's Word has to say—if anything—about near-death experiences.

Are Near-Death Experiences Biblical?

It's easy to quickly dismiss near-death experiences as nothing more than imaginations gone wild. After all, NDEs are uncommon, and the experiences almost always tend toward the sensational. So, how do we really judge whether someone's near-death experience is real? How do we know that chemical reactions in the brain, under stressful situations, aren't fooling NDErs into thinking that they've actually gone to heaven? Certain drugs have been known to alter brain chemistry and give the impression of an out-of-body experience. And since we know our enemy, Satan, is a liar and deceiver, could it be that some (or all) NDEs are demonic in nature?

On the other hand, near-death stories often bring comfort to those struggling with the reality of their own death or the loss of a loved one. Should we deny them the truth that there is hope beyond death? And besides, what are we to think of those who have come to faith in Christ after having a near-death experience? Shouldn't we celebrate their salvation? And what about Christians who have experienced NDEs and, as a result, started living more God-centered lives? Why would we want to say anything that would diminish their newfound enthusiasm?

A friend who served with me on our staff for many years had an experience during a traumatic illness in which he came to heaven's gate but God prevented him from entering. This experience was so real to him that after he recovered he made some dramatic decisions that impacted every aspect of his life. This is a man of deep faith with a seminary degree who is well versed in the Bible. Should I simply dismiss his experience because it sounds sensational?

Christian researcher J. Isamu Yamamoto, who has studied near-death experiences, cautions us to be careful not to dismiss NDEs out of hand but also not to unthinkingly accept them at face value:

> Since NDEs are of a subjective nature, determining their source is largely a speculative venture. With divine, demonic, and several natural factors all meriting consideration, a single, universal explanation for NDEs becomes quite risky.[8]

When it comes to near-death experiences we need to think biblically. This involves determining whether an NDE corroborates or contradicts Scripture, whether it glorifies God or self, and whether it motivates the experiencer to know more of God and His Word or to seek additional experiences. Specifically, we should keep seven principles in mind while evaluating the experiences of those who claim to have already visited heaven.

1. Near-Death Isn't Death

Nearly dead is not dead! As Miracle Max told Inigo Montoya in the movie *The Princess Bride*, "Your friend here is only *mostly* dead. There's a big difference between mostly dead and all dead. Mostly dead is slightly alive. With all dead, well . . . with all dead there's usually only one thing you can do. . . . Go through his clothes and look for loose change."[9]

The Bible is clear on this point: "Each person is destined to die *once* and after that comes judgment" (Heb. 9:27 NLT). I can hear the objections already: "What about the people in the Bible who died and were brought back to life, like Lazarus?" We'll consider their experiences in detail, but keep in mind that Lazarus, and others who underwent death twice, were rare exceptions and were brought back to life for unique reasons. Miracles occur—but they don't occur every day. If they did, they would be called "usuals." The point of Hebrews 9:27 is that, for the vast majority of humanity, God's plan is for them to die once and then face eternity.

Near-death experiences are just that: *near*-death, not *once-for-all-completely-dead* experiences. Therefore, the stories told by NDErs may tell us nothing more about life after death than someone who has traveled near my city of Dallas can tell us about such local landmarks as Thanksgiving Square, Klyde Warren Park, or Reunion Tower without ever actually being within the city limits. Both NDEs (near-Dallas experiences and near-death experiences) lack certitude. And in both cases reliable maps *are* available for those planning a journey to an unfamiliar destination. The only certain map for navigating eternity is the Bible. And that leads to a second important principle about evaluating NDEs.

2. *The Bible Is Sufficient*

Books like *Heaven Is for Real* and *To Heaven and Back* give the impression that the Bible is insufficient to tell us what we need to know about life after death. Though these books might bring comfort and hope to those who've lost loved ones, we should be very careful about turning away from the Word of God and toward some other source during times of grief and sadness. Remember what Alex Malarkey said: "The Bible is sufficient." And don't forget Paul's words of comfort to those who wondered what had happened to their loved ones who had died:

> But we do not want you to be uninformed, brethren, about those who are asleep, so that you will not grieve as do the rest who have no hope. For if we believe that Jesus died and rose again, even so God will bring with Him those who have fallen asleep in Jesus. For this we say to you by the word of the Lord, that we who are alive and remain until the coming of the Lord, will not precede those who have fallen asleep. For the Lord Himself will descend from heaven with a shout, with the voice of the archangel and with the trumpet of God, and the dead in Christ will rise first. Then we who are alive and remain will be caught up together with them in the clouds to meet the Lord in the air, and so we shall always be with the Lord. *Therefore comfort one another with these words.* (1 Thess. 4:13–18)

Paul is saying to the grieving Thessalonian Christians: "God does not want you to be ignorant of what has happened to your loved ones. Here is everything you need to know about what happens to a Christian after death."

Never in my ministry have I felt the need to turn to a book about near-death experiences to comfort the grieving, to bring hope to the hopeless, or to assure the doubtful. Hundreds and hundreds of times over the decades, I have looked into the faces of family members at a funeral service who had just experienced the sting of death and witnessed immediate relief as they heard the reassuring words of comfort from God's Word.

3. Adding to or Taking Away from the Bible Is Condemned

The Bible is eternal, inspired, and infallible. And because it is, God places inestimable value on His Word. For those who obey there are blessings; for those who disobey there are curses. The bookend of blessings and curses is easy to spot in the book of Revelation. The book opens with a blessing, "Blessed is he who reads and those who hear the words of the prophecy, and heed the things which are written in it" (Rev. 1:3), and ends with a curse:

> I testify to everyone who hears the words of the prophecy of this book: if anyone adds to them, God will add to him the plagues which are written in this book; and if anyone takes away from the words of the book of this prophecy, God will take away his part from the tree of life and from the holy city, which are written in this book. (22:18–19)

The book of Revelation is God's definitive answer to what awaits every person—Christian and non-Christian—after death. In this book, God tells us everything He wants us to know. Adding to, subtracting from, or twisting the truth

68

written in the book of Revelation is serious business and results in severe punishment.

Everyone who writes about heaven (including yours truly) should take this warning seriously. Unfortunately, many of the books and stories about near-death experiences—trips to heaven and coming back to tell the tale—come uncomfortably close to violating the warning in Revelation 22. For example, is the Holy Spirit *really* bluish in color, and does God the Father, whom no one has ever seen, *really* have wings as little four-year-old Colton Burpo claimed?[10]

4. Question the Identity of Any "Being of Light"

Not all who've had a near-death experience encountered a being of light, but those who have claim that being was Jesus Christ. However, many of these reports also claim that "Jesus" told them things contrary to the Word of God, such as:

"Sin isn't a problem."
"There is no hell."
"All people are welcomed into heaven."
"Every religion is equally true."

But how can this be if "Jesus Christ is the same yesterday and today and forever" (Heb. 13:8)? All of those statements contradict everything Jesus taught while He was on earth. It's impossible that these NDErs met the real Jesus, since He would never contradict His own Word. The only conclusion we can draw is that if these people experienced a legitimate near-death experience, the being they encountered was an antichrist—a counterfeit Christ.

J. Isamu Yamamoto anticipates the objection to such a declaration when he asks, "How can we conclude that this being of light is an evil spirit when he exudes love and joy and peace, and when he encourages people to love others?" Good question—and Yamamoto provides a good answer:

It is tough to speak against such an argument. It is much easier to speak against a horned demon with a pitchfork who commands people to hate, hurt, and rebel. Spiritual warfare, however, is a battleground where it is often difficult to identify the enemy. Frequently he disguises himself as a beloved friend. Deception has always been this way, and it has been a deadly weapon in his arsenal evident since he used it in the Garden of Eden. Indeed, Paul warned Timothy that "in later times some will abandon the faith and follow deceiving spirits and things taught by demons" (1 Tim. 4:1). Of course, the most evil deception is when the Devil appears to be God. Again, Paul's words ring true: "Satan himself masquerades as an angel of light" (2 Cor. 11:14).[11]

Satan's strategy is similar to that of terrorists who disguise themselves as civilian noncombatants, making it difficult for allied soldiers to distinguish friend from foe. If Satan or his demons can deceive someone through disguise—wearing the mask of Christ to cover the heart of antichrist—then the result is one less person bound for heaven.

To make matters worse, popular thinker Dinesh D'Souza observed, "We interpret our experiences through a cultural lens." In other words, we see what we want to see. "A Christian may see a radiant being and say it's Jesus," D'Souza argues, "while a Muslim might say it's Muhammad. Since no one knows what either Jesus or Muhammad looked like—and let's assume the radiant being isn't wearing a name tag—clearly the identification shows an element of cultural projection."[12] If this is true, then the veracity of those who claim to have had a near-death experience, traveled to heaven, and seen a being of light must be called into question. In heaven, the options as to the true identity of a being of light cannot be between Jesus and Muhammad. In heaven, there's only one option: Jesus.

5. Beware of the Occult

It is highly probable that those who have met a being of light during an NDE have met a demon impersonating Christ, leading to an experience with the occult and not an experience with God. It is a fact that near-death experiences often resemble out-of-body experiences reported by those who practice the occult. In both cases, people claim to have had otherworldly contacts and their worldview changed. They also claim to have developed psychic powers like clairvoyance (the ability to see something about the past, present, or future beyond natural means) and telepathy (the ability to receive or send thoughts from and to another person).

For example, Diane Corcoran, the president of the International Association for Near-Death Studies (IANDS), emphasized in her opening remarks to the 2014 annual conference in Newport Beach, California, that the long-term psychic effects of a near-death experience are just as important as the experience itself. As Gideon Lichfield, who covered the conference for *The Atlantic* magazine, wrote:

Many people, [Corcoran] said, don't realize for years that they've had an NDE, and piece it together only after they notice the effects. These include heightened sensitivity to light, sound, and certain chemicals; becoming more caring and generous, sometimes to a fault; having trouble with time-keeping and finances; feeling unconditional love for everyone, which can be taxing on relatives and friends; and having a strange influence on electrical equipment. At one conference of NDErs, Corcoran recounted, the hotel's computer system went down. "You put 400 experiencers in a hotel together, *something's* gonna happen," she said.[13]

Of course Ms. Corcoran didn't mean that someone accidentally kicked the plug from the wall. Rather, she is suggesting that the psychosomatic energy of the four hundred NDErs frazzled the hotel's computers. If this actually happened, the power behind such an occurrence is attributable to the kingdom of darkness rather than God's kingdom of light.

Occultism and any hint of occultism is a clear violation of Scripture—both in the Old Testament and the New Testament—and should be avoided like the spiritual plague that it is.[14]

6. Jesus's Death and Resurrection Should Be Central to Any Revelation from God

Some people argued that Saul (Paul) had an NDE when he fell to the ground and saw a blinding light at his conversion. Here's how Luke described Saul's experience:

As he was traveling, it happened that he was approaching Damascus, and suddenly a light from heaven flashed around him; and he fell to the ground and heard a voice saying to him, "Saul, Saul, why are you persecuting Me?" And he said, "Who are You, Lord?" And He said, "I am Jesus whom you are persecuting, but get up and enter the city, and it will be told you what you must do." (Acts 9:3–6)

For NDErs, Saul's conversion mirrors a near-death experience: the vision of a bright light, encountering Jesus, the transformation of Saul's life, and the charge of insanity—just as NDErs are sometimes labeled. However, there are a number of problems with this conclusion.

First, Paul was very much alive and nowhere near death at his conversion. Second, the light was something unlike a typical NDE because it literally blinded Paul until he later recovered. Third, in telling King Agrippa of his experience, Paul never mentioned anything remotely resembling a near-death experience. Finally, unlike the Jesus of typical near-death experiences, the Jesus Paul encountered commissioned him to evangelize exclusively in His name—to bring people to repentance and to humble themselves under the lordship of Christ.[15]

It is this last point that is particularly important. While it's true that some who claim to have had a near-death experience have subsequently come to faith in Christ and kept the death and resurrection of Jesus at the center of their story, most NDErs keep the focus of their experience on *themselves* or on some nondescript heavenly being. This wasn't the case with Paul—from the moment he encountered Jesus on the road to Damascus until he drew his last breath, his focus was on Jesus Christ—the exclusive Son of God. Paul summed up his life's mission when he told the Corinthian believers: "I determined to know nothing among you except Jesus Christ, and Him crucified" (1 Cor. 2:2). Any story of near death that excludes Jesus Christ and His exclusive message of salvation for those who trust Him is highly suspect.

7. *The Bible Doesn't Record Near-Death Experiences*

The real question when evaluating any near-death experience is, "Does the Bible record any NDEs?" Some say yes, citing the examples of Lazarus, Jesus, Stephen, Paul, and John. We'll examine the experience of each of these men, but before we do let me make one point perfectly clear: in the past God occasionally raised people from the dead (meaning they were actually dead!) to illustrate a spiritual truth. God stopped raising people from the dead sometime during the New Testament era because this miracle was no longer needed to affirm the veracity of the apostles' message. Once the New Testament was completed, the test of any self-proclaimed messenger from God was his adherence to the Bible, not his ability to raise people from the dead. And that same test applies today.

Nevertheless, here are some examples of God bringing the dead back to life before the completion of the New Testament:

- Elijah and the widow of Zarephath's son (1 Kings 17:17–24)
- Elisha and the Shunammite woman's son (2 Kings 4:18–37)
- Ezekiel and the valley of dry bones (Ezek. 37:1–14)
- Jesus and Jairus's daughter (Matt. 9:18–19, 23–26; Mark 5:22–24, 35–43; Luke 8:41–42, 49–56)

- Jesus and the widow of Nain's son (Luke 7:11–15)
- Peter and Tabitha (Acts 9:36–43)
- Paul and Eutychus (Acts 20:6–12)
- Unnamed saints (Heb. 11:35)

Yet none of these examples qualifies as a near-death experience because no individual reported what he or she saw on the other side of death—a basic requirement for an NDE.

Consider the dramatic story of Lazarus, whom Jesus brought back to life after he had been dead for four days (John 11:17, 39, 43–44). Nowhere in the biblical record did John give an account of what Lazarus saw, heard, or experienced in heaven.

Of course, Jesus is the ultimate example of Someone who returned from the dead. All four Gospels agree on this point: Jesus died, was buried, and after three days was raised from the dead. But while Jesus hung on the cross approaching death, He experienced none of the typical near-death experiences. He had no incoherent out-of-body experience, He didn't travel through a tunnel toward a light, and He certainly didn't have an overwhelming sense of peace.

Rather, Jesus was cognizant and rational, forgiving those who condemned Him to the cross, promising one of the criminals a home in Paradise, speaking to His mother and His disciple John, praying to the Father, and surrendering His spirit. After His resurrection from the dead (not the "nearly dead"), Jesus didn't reveal any information about His experience in heaven. Instead, He prepared His disciples for the mission that lay before them, "speaking of the things concerning the kingdom of God" (Acts 1:3).

The stoning of Stephen is perhaps the closest thing to a near-death experience recorded in the Bible.

> Now when [the Jewish officials, the Sanhedrin] heard [Stephen's speech condemning them], they were cut to the quick, and they began gnashing their teeth at him. But being full of the Holy Spirit, he gazed intently into heaven and saw the glory of God, and Jesus standing at the right hand of God; and he said, "Behold, I see the heavens opened up and the Son of Man standing at the right hand of God." (Acts 7:54–56)

Some of the elements of an NDE were present in Stephen's case: an encounter with Jesus, seeing God, and witnessing the gates of heaven opening wide. Nevertheless, there are key aspects in Stephen's situation that prevent it from being classified as a near-death experience.

First, Stephen's vision of heaven and Jesus takes place before his stoning began. If Stephen's experience was a true NDE, we'd expect the vision to come just before death, after being pummeled by the stones. Second, the Scripture is clear that Stephen received his vision of Jesus and heaven because he was "full of the Holy Spirit," meaning that the Spirit of God granted him the vision to peer into the heavenly realm. I rarely hear people who claim NDEs attribute those experiences to the Holy Spirit.

Third, Stephen's vision was not unlike the visions given to Isaiah, Ezekiel, and Daniel—none of whom were near death when they saw scenes of heavenly splendor. Fourth, when Stephen was close to the moment of his death, the writer's focus was not on Stephen's vision of Jesus and heaven but on his prayer of surrender and forgiveness.

They went on stoning Stephen as he called on the Lord and said, "Lord Jesus, receive my spirit!" Then falling on his knees, he cried out with a loud voice, "Lord, do not hold this sin against them!" Having said this, he fell asleep. (vv. 59–60)

Finally—Stephen actually died instead of "nearly died." I can't emphasize strongly enough that the Bible does not record people who died (or "nearly died"), took a brief tour of heaven, and then returned from wherever they were to write a bestselling book about their experiences.

"But didn't the apostle Paul admit to having such an experience?" some might wonder. It is true that the famed apostle was "caught up to the third heaven" (2 Cor. 12:2), which some people equate with a near-death experience. Yet two important factors disqualify this as an NDE.

First, there is no indication that Paul was close to death when the experience occurred. The apostle confessed he didn't know whether his trip to heaven was physical ("in the body") or metaphysical ("apart from the body"), but it's clear that Paul hadn't died or almost died.

Second, Paul did not reveal any details about his experience or vision of heaven. He was instructed not to speak of what he saw and heard. If Christianity's greatest theologian, who wrote nearly half of the New Testament, was prohibited from publishing a firsthand account of his trip to heaven, why would God authorize someone today to pen such a book? It's certainly a question worthy of consideration. If anyone was allowed to write about their experience in heaven after having nearly died, we'd assume it would be Paul.

What does all of this mean? Very simply, there are no biblical accounts of the kind of near-death experiences we hear so much about today. And while I would never say that God is incapable of granting—or unwilling to ever grant— someone that experience, the weight of Scripture seems to argue against NDEs.

Skeptics claim that near-death experiences are no more real than alien abductions, psychic powers, or poltergeists— fodder for charlatans looking to make a quick dollar off the gullible and foolish. To skeptics, NDErs are no better than snake-oil salespersons.

And while we need not be as cynical as the run-of-the-mill skeptic about NDEs, there is good evidence to question any-one claiming to have had a near-death experience and telling us that heaven is really real. We already know that, because Jesus has promised He is preparing a place for us in heaven.

Everything you need to know about that thrilling "place called heaven" is revealed in the Bible—and in the pages that follow you will discover many stirring and surprising truths from God's Word about your future home.

4

Do Christians Immediately Go to Heaven When They Die?

While we are at home in the body we are absent from the Lord . . . and prefer rather to be absent from the body and to be at home with the Lord.

2 Corinthians 5:6, 8

In the dead of a Minnesota winter, a couple decided to thaw out on a Florida beach. But personal responsibilities kept the wife home an extra day, so she planned to fly down the day after her husband. When the husband arrived in Key West and checked in to the hotel, he unpacked and then shot off a quick email to his wife before going to the beach. Unfortunately, in his rush to get out the door he transposed two letters in his wife's email address.

Meanwhile, a minister's wife in Chicago had just buried her husband of forty-five years. Entering her home after the funeral, exhausted and numb from losing him so suddenly, she decided to check her email in hopes of reading messages of condolence to soothe her shattered spirit. Overlooking the address of the sender, she screamed when she saw the first message . . . and then fainted. Rushing into the room, her daughter saw her mother on the floor and revived her. Then the daughter read the message:

> *Darling Wife:*
>
> *I'm sure you're surprised to hear from me. I've just arrived and checked in, and I wanted to send you a quick note saying I can't wait until you get here. The staff has everything ready for you. I'm looking forward to seeing you tomorrow. And if everything goes as planned you should get here as quickly as I did.*
>
> *PS: It sure is hot down here. I know you're gonna love it!*

Theologian Reinhold Niebuhr once advised: "It is unwise for Christians to claim any knowledge of either the furniture of heaven or the temperature of hell."[1] And while there is some truth to Niebuhr's warning, I think we can safely assume that hell isn't anything like Key West!

We can also assume, based on what the Bible reveals about the new heaven and the new earth, that Key West—for all its beauty—doesn't hold a candle to the splendor of the future home God is preparing for us. But one thing is certain: every human being is going to either heaven or hell when they die.

In his book *Heaven*, Randy Alcorn observes that "world-wide, 3 people die every second, 180 every minute, and nearly 11,000 every hour. If the Bible is right about what happens to us after death, it means that more than 250,000 people every day go either to Heaven or Hell."[2] The mind staggers at those statistics—a quarter of a million spirits depart the earth, every single day, bound for one of two destinies. Numbers like this prove the accuracy of the old adage: "No one gets out of this world alive." But why is death inevitable—both for Christians and non-Christians?

Why the Living Must Die

Death is the result of the universal disease infecting us all: sin. Solomon declared that death is the "fate for all men" (Eccles. 9:3)—"for the righteous and for the wicked . . . for the clean and for the unclean . . . [for the] good man [and for] the sinner" (v. 2). The universality of death is illustrated at every funeral and in every cemetery throughout the world. J. Sidlow Baxter was correct when he wrote:

> A million graveyards proclaim with ceaseless voice that man is mortal and that the living are dying. What wreckage of the race has Death made! What is this revolving orb on which we live but the vast cemetery of mankind?[3]

Death is every person's fate because every man, woman, and child is guilty of sin against God. "For all have sinned and fall short of the glory of God," Paul declared in Romans 3:23. And sin—the thumbing of our noses at God's moral code—is punishable by death, just as Paul wrote later in his letter to the Romans: "For the wages of sin is death" (6:23).

From the very beginning of human history, death was the just punishment for sin. God warned Adam and Eve that if they rebelled against His clear command not to eat from the tree of the knowledge of good and evil, they would die. And die they did.

With the exceptions of Enoch and Elijah (and those believers alive at the rapture of the church), every person since Adam and Eve has died or will die. The fact that death awaits us all strikes fear into the hearts of many people. Job called death "the king of terrors" (Job 18:14). The psalmist confessed that his heart was in agony because "the terrors of death have fallen upon me" (Ps. 55:4). And the writer to the Hebrews likened death to a slave master, chaining humanity in fear (Heb. 2:15).

Death is the nightmare of all nightmares for those who face death without faith in Jesus Christ. The actor Jack Nicholson knows the terror of death. He wrestled with his own mortality while making *The Bucket List*—a movie about two terminally ill men who leave a cancer ward for a road trip to do the things they always wanted to do before "kicking the bucket." In an interview promoting the film, Nicholson said:

> I use to live so freely. The mantra for my generation was "Be your own man!" I always said, "Hey, you can have whatever rules you want—I'm going to have mine. I'll accept the guilt. I'll pay the check. I'll do the time." I chose my own way. That was my philosophical position well into my 50s. As I've gotten older, I've had to adjust. . . . We all want to go on

forever, don't we? We fear the unknown. Everybody goes to that wall, yet nobody knows what's on the other side. That's why we fear death.[4]

It's understandable for unbelievers to fear death—they don't know what awaits them on the other side of the grave. But even for believers, the prospects of death and dying can be unnerving. Joni Eareckson Tada wrote:

I look at my own degenerating body and wonder how I will approach that final passage. Will it be short and sweet? Or long and agonizing? Will my husband be able to take care of me? Or will my quadriplegia better suit me for a nursing home? It's not so much I'm afraid of death as dying.[5]

Without a doubt, the thought of death can fill us with terror and dread. However, knowing our destination when we depart this life can dramatically diminish that understandable fear.

Where the Dead Go When They Die

One of my mentors in seminary, Howard Hendricks, always encouraged his students to keep the hope of heaven at the center of our preaching because it is in heaven where life is found. He would say, "We are not in the land of the living on our way to the land of the dying. Instead, we are in the land of the dying on our way to the land of the living." How true that is!

For a Christian, death is not a terminus *of* life; death is a transition *to* life—real life. However, for the unbeliever, death marks a transition to what the Bible calls "the second death" (Rev. 20:14)—an eternal existence separated from God.

I believe every person born is presented with a choice at some point in his or her life: to either accept or reject God's free gift of salvation through Jesus Christ. It is a choice that can only be made in this life. Once we've passed through death's door into the afterlife, our choice is eternally fixed.

An epitaph on a century-old tombstone in an Indiana cemetery serves as a stark reminder of the certainty of death for all of us:

> Pause, stranger, when you pass me by;
> As you are now, so once was I.
> As I am now, so you will be,
> So prepare for death and follow me.

An unknown visitor to the cemetery saw the tombstone and, after a few moments in contemplation, scrawled a reply:

> To follow you I'm not content,
> Until I know which way you went.[6]

Whether you will die is not up for debate. The crucial question is this: "*Where* are you going after you die?" That question can only be answered by another question: "Did you trust in Jesus Christ for the forgiveness of your sins?" Your eternal destiny rests on your answer to that question.

Two Possible Destinations

The Bible employs various terms to describe the future destination of those who die—sheol, hades, Abraham's bosom, and Paradise—but ultimately there are only two destinies: heaven or hell.

However, as we saw in chapter 2, there is a present heaven—the "third heaven" of 2 Corinthians 12:2 where God dwells—and a future heaven that is being constructed for us as described in Revelation 21:1–2. The present heaven is the "temporary heaven" while the future heaven is the "permanent heaven." (We'll look at hell in greater detail in chapter 9, but, like heaven, there is both a temporary and a permanent place of suffering for the unsaved.)

Where Do Christians Go When They Die?

It is a great hope and comfort to know that at death the spirit of every believer is immediately ushered into the presence of God—the third heaven. And we have Jesus's promise to rely on for that assurance. He declared to the thief on the cross who, moments earlier, had professed his faith in Christ: "Truly I say to you, *today* you shall be with Me in Paradise" (Luke 23:43).

When Stephen was being stoned, he anticipated being with Jesus at death. Stephen "called on the Lord and said, 'Lord Jesus, receive my spirit!'" (Acts 7:59). Paul's great desire was "to depart and be with Christ" (Phil. 1:23). The Greek word for "depart" (*analuo*) was used in reference to a ship being loosed from its moorings so it might sail away. The "mooring" that kept Paul tethered to his earthly life was his commitment to the gospel ministry. But his ultimate desire was to "sail away" to Christ.

However, the most complete explanation of what happens to a believer the moment he or she dies is found in 2 Corinthians 5:6–8:

Therefore, being always of good courage, and knowing that while we are at home in the body we are absent from the Lord—for we walk by faith, not by sight—we are of good courage, I say, and prefer rather to be absent from the body and to be at home with the Lord.

Without getting lost in the grammatical weeds of the original language, let me point out two important insights from the Greek. First, the phrases in verse 6, "we are at home in the body" and "we are absent from the Lord," are in the present tense, representing continuous action. We might paraphrase verse 6 like this: "Therefore, being always of good courage, and knowing that while we are *continuing* to live at home in the body we likewise are *continuing* to live absent from the Lord."

In other words, while our bodies are here on earth, we're not in the presence of Christ in heaven, any more than I am in my home with my wife, Amy, in Dallas while I am also in a lonely hotel room in New York. Guess where I would rather be?

Second, the phrases "to be absent from the body" and "to be at home with the Lord" indicate actions that are completed rather than continuing. We might paraphrase verse 8 like this: "we are of good courage, I say, and prefer rather to have completely departed from the body and to be *finally* at home with the Lord."

That is exactly how I feel when I've been away from home too long. I'm ready to be completely absent from New York (or wherever I happened to be) and to be finally at home with Amy.

When I'm away from home, I'm thinking about Amy and can't wait to get back to her. But once I'm home, I certainly don't long to be in that lonely hotel room in an unfamiliar city. That's the point Paul is making in 2 Corinthians 5:6, 8. To be present here (earth) is to be absent from there (heaven), but to be absent here is to be present there. Once we leave our earthly bodies behind—which are nothing more than the cocoon from which a butterfly emerges—our spirits are instantly transported to our heavenly home where Christ is, as we await the time we will receive our eternal bodies. More about that in the next section.

The Third Heaven: Our Real but Temporary Home

Until the new heaven and the new earth are completed, all Christians who die are immediately transported into the presence of God—the third heaven. The apostle Paul is clear that at the rapture all Christians will receive their new, glorified bodies in which they will live for eternity. "All Christians" includes those Christians who died prior to the rapture ("the dead in Christ," as Paul calls them), as well as those Christians who are alive at the rapture and never experience death:

> For the Lord Himself will descend from heaven with a shout, with the voice of the archangel and with the trumpet of God, and the dead in Christ will rise first. Then we who are alive and remain will be caught up together with them in the clouds to meet the Lord in the air, and so we shall always be with the Lord. Therefore comfort one another with these words. (1 Thess. 4:16–18)

Paul describes the instantaneous change that both the "dead in Christ" and those Christians alive at the rapture will experience:

> Behold, I tell you a mystery; we will not all sleep, but we will all be changed, in a moment, in the twinkling of an eye, at the last trumpet; for the trumpet will sound, and the dead will be raised imperishable, and we will be changed. (1 Cor. 15:51–52)

Not every Christian will die (or "sleep," as Paul describes what happens to the Christian's physical body at death) but all Christians—both those who are alive at the time of the rapture and every believer who has died since the time of Christ—will receive a new incorruptible and imperishable body that is designed for eternity.

One interesting question people often ask is about the physical state of those Christians who die *before* the rapture. Are they simply disembodied spirits who are ushered into the presence of the Lord, or do they receive some kind of temporary bodies until they receive their permanent, new bodies at the rapture?

Some writers such as Randy Alcorn believe Christians will be given temporary bodies when they die before receiving their resurrected, glorified, and eternal bodies at the rapture. Alcorn writes:

> Given the consistent physical descriptions of the present Heaven [a term referring to the third heaven, where God is] and those who dwell there, it seems possible—though this is certainly debatable—that between our earthly life and our bodily resurrection, God may grant us some physical form that will allow us to function as human beings while in that unnatural state "between bodies," awaiting our resurrection.[7]

God created us body, soul, and spirit, not just soul and spirit. There has never been a time when we existed without a physical body. Before our conception in our mother's womb we didn't exist at all. But at our conception, when God breathed life into us, He gave us a body.

Furthermore, we will also exist in bodily form rather than as disembodied spirits in the new heaven and the new earth. These "made for eternity" bodies will be given to us at the rapture of the church. Thus, the reasoning goes, if we have always existed in bodily form in the past and will also inhabit physical bodies in the future, why would we exist only in spirit form during the relatively brief span of time between our death and the rapture?

The Bible does not definitively answer the question of whether Christians receive a temporary body before the rapture, but as we will see in the next section, the story Jesus told in Luke 16 about the experience of Lazarus and the rich man provides a strong clue to that question's answer.

Where Did the Old Testament Saints Go When They Died?

If Christians since the time of Christ go immediately to heaven when they die, where did those believers who lived before Christ go when they died? This is a little more complicated and debatable than answering the question concerning Christians who die today.

First, we need to understand who qualified as an Old Testament believer, or "saint," as some people call them. An Old Testament saint was anyone—Jewish or Gentile—whom God declared "righteous." In my book *Not All Roads Lead to Heaven*, I explain in depth that all believers—whether they lived before Christ or after Christ—are saved the same way: by the death of Jesus Christ. For those who lived before Christ, His payment for their sin was "credited" to their account the moment they exercised faith in God's revelation. Abraham lived thousands of years before Christ, yet "he believed in the LORD; and He accounted it to him for righteousness" (Gen. 15:6 NKJV).

Second, it's important to understand two important biblical terms that refer to the place of the dead: the Hebrew word *sheol* and the Greek word *hades*. Both words mean roughly the same thing: "covered" or "hidden." According to some scholars *sheol* is divided into two compartments: Paradise (or "Abraham's bosom") where the righteous reside, and a place of torment called hades where the unrighteous reside. According to these scholars, the best illustration of this division between Abraham's bosom and the place of torment is found in Luke 16:19–26:

> Now there was a rich man, and he habitually dressed in purple and fine linen, joyously living in splendor every day. And a poor man named Lazarus was laid at his gate, covered with sores, and longing to be fed with the crumbs which were falling from the rich man's table; besides, even the dogs were coming and licking his sores. Now the poor man died and was carried away by the angels to Abraham's bosom; and the rich man also died and was buried. In Hades he lifted up his eyes, being in torment, and saw Abraham far away and Lazarus in his bosom. And he cried out and said, "Father Abraham, have mercy on me, and send Lazarus so that he may dip the tip of his finger in water and cool off my

tongue, for I am in agony in this flame." But Abraham said, "Child, remember that during your life you received your good things, and likewise Lazarus bad things; but now he is being comforted here, and you are in agony. And besides all this, between us and you there is a great chasm fixed, so that those who wish to come over from here to you will not be able, and that none may cross over from there to us."

Some people believe that given the amount of detail in this story—including the use of the name Lazarus (no other parable uses a proper name)—this is not a parable but the actual account of the deaths of two different men who experienced two different destinies. Whether this is a parable or not, Jesus uses this story to reveal some basic truths about the hereafter.

The most obvious principle in this story is all people do not experience the same destiny when they die. Some, like Lazarus, are ushered into a place of peace while others, like the rich man, immediately begin to experience horrific suffering. Notice that the division between comfort and agony centered on being in or being away from Abraham's presence or "bosom." For the Old Testament believer, being in the presence of the beloved father of the Jewish people was synonymous with being in the presence of God Himself. For so-called New Testament saints and sinners—those who either accepted or rejected God's grace in the crucifixion and resurrection of Christ—the afterlife centers on being in or apart from Jesus's presence.

As I said earlier, some biblical scholars believe that "Abraham's bosom" was one of two divisions of this holding place for the dead called sheol that was reserved for those believers who died before the resurrection of Jesus Christ—such as Lazarus in Jesus's story. After having been carried away by angels to Abraham's side, Lazarus found comfort, blessing, and intimate fellowship with the Old Testament patriarch.

But to me this description sounds very much like the present (third) heaven where God is rather than one-half of a "duplex" that houses believers and unbelievers. After all, Abraham's bosom was said to be "far away" from hades (the place of torment for unbelievers), not an adjoining compartment. Also, Jesus promised the repentant thief—who died before Jesus's resurrection—he would be with the Lord—not just Abraham—in Paradise (Luke 23:43).

Additionally, the weight of Scripture supports the interpretation that Abraham's bosom is heaven. For example, it is strongly implied that faithful Enoch was transported directly to heaven and not to a holding place in sheol or hades, when God "took him" (Gen. 5:24; Heb. 11:5). Furthermore, 2 Kings 2:1 and 2:11 clearly say Elijah was taken "by a whirlwind *to heaven*." Moreover, David believed God would not "abandon [his] soul to Sheol," but would give him "fullness of joy" in God's presence (Ps. 16:10–11).

David also prayed that after "all the days of [his life]," he would "dwell in the house of the LORD forever" (23:6). That can only refer to one place: heaven. Finally, David's son Solomon observed in Ecclesiastes 12:7: "The dust will return to the earth as it was, and the spirit will return to God who gave it." In other words, Old Testament believers' bodies would decay and return as dust to the earth, but their spirits would continue to live in the presence of God—also known as "Abraham's bosom."

Where Do Unbelievers Go When They Die?

As we've seen, Old Testament and New Testament believers immediately enter the presence of the Lord when they die. They are very much alive and aware that they are in a place we refer to as the "third heaven" as they await the new heaven and new earth, in which they will reside for eternity.

But what happens to unbelievers when they die? According to Jesus's story of the rich man and Lazarus, they are immediately dispatched to hades—a place of unbearable pain and agony. Hades is the immediate, but temporary, destination of non-Christians when they die. Let me explain what I mean by "temporary."

Just as Abraham's bosom or "the third heaven" is not the eternal destiny of believers, hades is not the final destiny of unbelievers. Instead, hades is a holding place for unbelievers as they await the resurrection of their bodies for the great white throne judgment, as described in Revelation 20:11–15:

> Then I saw a great white throne and Him who sat upon it, from whose presence earth and heaven fled away, and no place was found for them. And I saw the dead, the great and the small, standing before the throne, and books were opened; and another book was opened, which is the book of life; and the dead were judged from the things which were written in the books, according to their deeds. And the sea gave up the dead which were in it, and death and Hades gave up the dead which were in them; and they were judged, every one of them according to their deeds. Then death and Hades were thrown into the lake of fire. This is the second death, the lake of fire. And if anyone's name was not found written in the book of life, he was thrown into the lake of fire.

The lake of fire (also referred to as *gehenna* in the Bible) is the eternal destination for all unbelievers, just as the new heaven and new earth is the eternal destination for all believers. Just as the third (or present) heaven is the temporary destination for believers as they await the new heaven and new earth, hades is the temporary destination for all unbelievers as they await the eternal lake of fire.

Neither the third heaven nor hades is any kind of neutral "waiting station" for the dead. Although hades is only a temporary location for unbelievers, it is a place of indescribable suffering. Just as believers begin to immediately and consciously experience the comfort of being in God's presence when they die, unbelievers begin to immediately experience the horrendous suffering of being separated from God at the moment of their death.

Notice how the rich man in Jesus's story begs for mercy and asks whether Lazarus might come from heaven and "dip the tip of his finger in water and cool off my tongue, for I am in agony in this flame" (Luke 16:24). The rich man's request is filled with irony. During life, he knew of Lazarus and his suffering. Unable to buy food, or even fend off the dogs that came to lick his sores, Lazarus sat at the rich man's gate every day, begging for a few crumbs of food from the rich man's table (vv. 20–21). Yet the rich man did not lift a finger to relieve Lazarus's misery.

However, after he died, the rich man couldn't buy relief for himself. He's reduced to begging for mercy from the one he mistreated in life. The rich man reaped in death what he had sown in life, just as Jacob Marley did in Charles Dickens's *A Christmas Carol*. Marley's ghost lamented to Scrooge, "I wear the chain I forged in life. . . . I made it link by link, and yard by yard; I girded it on my own free will, and of my own free will I wore it."[8] And so it is with all who measure life according to self and not according to the Savior. Jesus said, "by your standard of measure it will be measured to you in return" (Luke 6:38). And what was measured to the rich man was "agony"—*odynaomai*, meaning continual pain and grief.

But the rich man was mistaken in thinking that Lazarus could leave Abraham's side and become a minister of mercy in hades. Even if Abraham had wanted to dispatch Lazarus to minister to the rich man he would have been unable to. God established an impenetrable barrier between the righteous and unrighteous—"a great chasm fixed" (16:26)—preventing those in heaven to travel to hades and those in hades to travel to heaven, thereby eliminating any possibility of salvation after death.

In fact, "the Lord knows how . . . to keep the unrighteous under punishment for the day of judgment" (2 Pet. 2:9). "Keep" is in the present tense, indicating that the wicked are held captive continuously, as a guard keeps careful watch over a condemned prisoner on death row. Once unbelievers die and are held for final judgment, their fate is fixed.

However, the rich man was not completely heartless—even in hades. Not wanting his brothers who were still living to experience his suffering, he pleaded with Abraham to send Lazarus to his five brothers to warn them about what awaited them unless they repented. But again, Abraham refused. The brothers had the Scripture, which provided all the information they needed about salvation.

But the rich man refused to take no for an answer, and stated his brothers would only believe if they had a miraculous sign of someone coming back from the grave. Abraham countered, "If they do not listen to Moses and the Prophets, they will not be persuaded even if someone [like Lazarus] rises from the dead" (Luke 16:31). These words from Jesus proved to be prophetic, for even when Jesus returned from the dead the vast majority of people continued in their unbelief.

Heaven or Hell: A Forever Choice

Here's the basic truth Jesus's story of Lazarus and the rich man reveals about what happens when we die: either we *immediately* begin experiencing the eternal bliss of being in God's presence or we *immediately* begin experiencing the unending horror of being separated from God.

It's true that at some future time after death, Christians will change locations from the third heaven—the presence of the Lord—to the new heaven and the new earth. Likewise, unbelievers will also experience a change of address after the great white throne judgment, moving from the place of temporary suffering (hades) to the place of eternal torment (the lake of fire).

But both cases are nothing more than a change of location and are not a change in experience. The most fundamental truth Jesus reveals in this story is that the moment we die our eternal destiny is sealed—forever.

As you contemplate whether you are traveling on the road leading to heaven or hell, consider these sobering words from my friend Erwin Lutzer:

> Five minutes after you die you will either have had your first glimpse of heaven with its euphoria and bliss or your first genuine experience of unrelenting horror and regret.

Either way, your future will be irrevocably fixed and eternally unchangeable.

In those first moments, you will be more alive than you ever have been. Vivid memories of your friends and your life on planet earth will be mingled with a daunting anticipation of eternity. You will have had your first direct glimpse of Christ or your first encounter with evil as you have never known it. And it will be too late to change your address.[9]

If you wait until the moment you die to choose your eternal destination, you will have waited one second too long.

5

What Will We Do in Heaven?

Well done, good and faithful servant; you have been faithful
over a few things, I will make you ruler over many things.
Enter into the joy of your lord.

Matthew 25:23 NKJV

At a dinner party, guests were discussing the possibilities of
future rewards and punishments after death. Sam remained
quiet, which was unusual for him since he was a born talker.
Not wanting him to feel excluded from the conversation, his
hostess turned and asked his views on heaven and hell. "I
don't want to express an opinion," Sam said. "It's a policy
for me to keep silent. You see, I have friends in both places."[1]

"Sam" was Samuel Clemens, better known as Mark Twain,
and in truth he spoke often of both places. For example, in
one speech, Twain joked:

The election makes me think of a story of a man who was dying. He had only two minutes to live, so he sent for a clergyman and asked him, "Where is the best place to go to?" He was undecided about it. So the minister told him that each place had its advantages—heaven for climate, and hell for society.[2]

Twain's tongue-in-cheek story illustrates a lie many have embraced about heaven: it will be a place of perpetual boredom, populated by boring people.

Three Popular Myths about God and Heaven

Science-fiction writer and atheist Isaac Asimov also embraced that belief, once remarking, "I don't believe in the afterlife, so I don't have to spend my whole life fearing hell, or fearing heaven even more. For whatever the tortures of hell, I think the boredom of heaven would be even worse."[3]

You and I might agree with that conclusion if we believed some of the common myths about God, heaven, and eternity.

Myth #1: God Is a Cosmic Killjoy

Mark Twain might joke that the advantage of heaven is the climate and the advantage of hell is the company, but heaven and hell are no laughing matter. Believe it or not, many people—like Isaac Asimov—have made decisions about their eternal destiny based on where they think the real never-ending party is going to occur. These people view God as a perennial party pooper and Satan as the life of the party. Those who've come to that conclusion are convinced that heaven must be as dull as watching paint dry, while hell must be as exhilarating as driving in a NASCAR race. Yet both of those flawed conclusions are based on basic misunderstandings about both God and Satan.

Have you ever been stuck at a dinner party seated next to a hopelessly boring personality? Minutes seem like hours and you are convinced the evening will never end. Satan is that kind of companion. There really is nothing interesting about him. He has never created anything in his entire existence. Who would want to be stuck with him for eternity?

But there is nothing boring about God. He is exceedingly and eternally fascinating: just look at the present world He has created for us to live in. Heaven is the place where everything will be eternally good, beautiful, enjoyable, refreshing, fascinating, and exciting because heaven's Creator is all of those things.

Myth #2: Heaven Will Be Monotonous

Some people are convinced that no matter how exciting the activities of heaven may be, doing the same thing over and over for eternity will become monotonous. "Too much of a good thing isn't good, it's boring," is their motto.

But the problem isn't heaven—the problem is us. A friend of mine used to tell her children whenever they complained of being bored that "only boring people get bored." It wasn't that my friend's kids didn't have enough to do—they had a house full of video games, televisions, movies, board games, sports equipment, pets, and friends; they just got tired of doing the same things every day. It is ironic that any child (or adult for that matter) in America could play with thousands of dollars' worth of video equipment and be more bored with life than a child in Africa playing with two sticks and a stone.

The truth is we can't handle the monotony of life on earth—even if it comes packaged as fun and games—so we assume life in heaven is just as monotonous and boring. But monotony doesn't have to be boring, as G. K. Chesterton pointed out:

> A child kicks his legs rhythmically through excess, not absence, of life. Because children have abounding vitality, because they are in spirit fierce and free, therefore they want things repeated and unchanged. They always say, "Do it again"; and the grown-up person does it again until he is nearly dead. For grown-up people are not strong enough to exult in monotony. But perhaps God is strong enough to exult in monotony. It is possible that God says every morning, "Do it again" to the sun; and every evening, "Do it again" to the moon. . . . It may be that He has the eternal appetite of infancy; for we have sinned and grown old, and our Father is younger than we.[4]

The activities of heaven will never get monotonous—even if we do them over and over—because we will no longer inhabit aging bodies that grow tired or live in a sin-infected world that makes life tedious. In that "placed called heaven" we will enjoy an "excess of life." We'll be like children saying to our heavenly Father, "Do it again!"

Myth #3: Heaven Will Be One Long Church Service

The idea that heaven is an eternal worship service is a persistent one. A number of years ago we had a guest preacher at our church who said, "If you have trouble sitting through a two-hour worship service here on earth, you will be miserable in heaven because all we are going to do for eternity is praise God." I groaned when I heard that because it made heaven sound like a giant yawn-fest—as evidenced by the very few "Amens" from the audience.

Now don't get me wrong. I'm a pastor who loves to sing God's praises with His people. However, although we were created by God for worship, we were also created to do *more* than worship.

While worshiping God will be a central activity in heaven, it will not be our only activity. Just as Christians today can offer praise to God while engaging in other tasks throughout the week, Christians in the new heaven and new earth will worship God during special, designated times as well as while involved in other activities.

Two Primary Responsibilities: Worship and Work

When God created Adam, He gave him two primary responsibilities: to work and to worship. Scripture says that "the LORD God planted a garden toward the east, in Eden; and there He placed the man whom He had formed," in order "to cultivate it and keep it" (Gen. 2:8, 15). That was the work Adam was to accomplish.

But Adam was also created to worship God. Genesis 3:8 implies that Adam and Eve had daily fellowship with the Lord—they walked with Him "in the cool of the day." When Christ establishes our eternal home on the new earth, it will be an Eden-like existence. And just as Adam had two primary responsibilities in Eden, we will have two primary responsibilities in the new heaven and new earth.

Exhilarating Worship Like You've Never Experienced

One of the most remarkable aspects of our worship in heaven will be seeing Jesus face-to-face. Our response to that experience will be unlike anything we've ever known on earth. Perhaps this insight might help you catch a glimpse about what our worship experience will be like in that "place called heaven."

We know the angelic host ceaselessly worships the Father and the Son with shouts of praise. According to John, the number of angels probably numbers in the hundreds of millions—"myriads of myriads, and thousands of thousands" (Rev. 5:11). The sound must be unlike anything heard on earth.

Just a few years ago, fans of the Seattle Seahawks football team set a world record as the loudest fans in the NFL. On December 2, 2013, during a third-down defensive stand against the New Orleans Saints, the Seahawks fans produced an ear-splitting 137.6 decibels. (The roar of a jet engine one hundred feet away produces 140 decibels.) The Seahawks fans' "praise" was so loud it triggered a minor earthquake![5]

A crowd of screaming football fanatics is no match for the "heavenly fans" that are right now praising God in the third heaven. Occasionally, I hear complaints from church members about the music in our services being "too loud." Well, the worship in heaven is not going to be some soft, contemplative, private experience. How do I know that? Look at Isaiah's description of the angelic worship of God taking place right now in heaven:

> And the foundations of the thresholds [of the temple] trembled at the voice of [the angels] who called out [in worship to God]. (Isa. 6:4)

One day we will add our voices to that ground-shaking heavenly chorus of angels, shouting "Hallelujah!"—praise be to our God.

> I looked, and behold, a great multitude which no one could count, from every nation and all tribes and peoples and tongues, standing before the throne and before the Lamb, clothed in white robes, and palm branches were in their hands; and they cry out with a loud voice, saying, "Salvation to our God who sits on the throne, and to the Lamb." (Rev. 7:9–10)

The number and the sound of the worshipers in heaven will be unlike our worship on earth. But there's more to our heavenly worship than size and volume. In heaven no one will merely mouth the words or go through the motions of worship; all will sing with hearts ablaze. Worship in heaven will be spontaneous, genuine, and exhilarating. "Praise will not be something we will be assigned or commanded to do; it will be natural," Joni Eareckson Tada wrote. "A supernatural effervescent response of the born-again creature, new and fit for heaven."[6]

If you've ever had that incredible experience in a worship service in which the expressions of your lips truly represented the adoration of your heart, you understand what Joni is describing. And rather than being a rare exception to the otherwise rote and programmed activity too many church-goers engage in most Sundays, the kind of worship that flows out of the deepest recesses of our hearts will happen every time we are in God's presence in the new heaven and new earth.

But in the new heaven and new earth, worship will not be limited to formal times of praising God. Randy Alcorn asked whether we will "always be engaged in worship."[7] The answer is yes and no, depending on your definition of worship. If you limit worship to praising God, praying, and preaching, then the answer is no. We will be involved in an array of other activities beyond formalized worship.

On the other hand, if you define worship as Paul did, then the answer is yes. Paul wrote, "Whether, then, you eat or drink or whatever you do, do all to the glory of God" (1 Cor. 10:31). In other words, we should worship God when we sit down for a meal, converse with our spouse or friend, play with our children or grandchildren, drive to work, or enjoy a vacation.

Worship is a continual awareness of, gratitude toward, and submission to God in everything we do. God is honored with my worship while I'm enjoying dinner with my daughters and thanking Him for them, sitting on a beach in Maui reflecting on His majestic power, or preparing for a difficult conversation and asking that I might reflect His point of view. We must quit thinking that we can only worship God while doing *nothing* else. Rather, we worship while doing *everything* else.

Invigorating Work That You Actually Enjoy

God is a worker. He did not create the world and then retire (though He did take one day off). He worked before sin entered the world and continues to work while sin remains in the world. Jesus declared, "My Father is working until now, and I Myself am working" (John 5:17). Since we are created in the image of God, it should be no surprise that we have been created to work as well. Contrary to what many believe, work is not a "curse" from God as a result of Adam and Eve's sin in the garden. Before the first couple ever took a bite of the forbidden fruit, God gave them the responsibility of work: "Then the LORD God took the man and put him into the garden of Eden to cultivate it and keep it" (Gen. 2:15).

Although Eden was perfect, it was not self-sustaining. God did His part in creating this slice of Paradise on earth, but He gave man the responsibility of cultivating it—tilling the soil and planting and harvesting crops. While it's true that Adam and Eve's work became much harder after their fall because of God's judgment, work has always been—and will always be—part of God's plan for each of us.

One of my best friends told me that when he was a teenager his dad would occasionally find him sitting on a sofa watching television. He said his father's response was always the same: "Get off that sofa and do something! What do you think you are—an international playboy?" Our heavenly Father did not create us to sit around and do nothing. That's why the whole concept of retirement today is flawed—it goes against God's basic plan for each one of us to do something productive with our lives. While we might cease working for the employer who provides us a paycheck, we are never to stop meaningful activity in order to sit around like international playboys.

Since our lives in the new heaven and the new earth are simply extensions of our lives now, we shouldn't be surprised that God plans for us to continue working in the new heaven and the new earth. Heaven will not be a place of eternal retirement where we do nothing but play golf or pluck a harp while living off a 401(k) plan that never runs dry.

"Wait a minute, working for eternity?" you ask. "That sounds more like hell than heaven!" The only reason we wince at the concept of working for eternity is because our labor has been burdened by the effects of sin's curse: bodies that grow tired, relationships that become strained, government regulations that are burdensome, and an environment that is uncooperative.

But in the new heaven and new earth all of those effects will evaporate because "there will no longer be any curse" (Rev. 22:3). In this world, work—no matter how much we enjoy it—can be exhausting. In the new world, work will be nothing but exhilarating.

Obviously, once the curse of sin is removed from the earth some jobs will automatically disappear. For example, there will be no need for doctors (disease will be eradicated), dentists (decay will be nonexistent), firefighters (destruction will be a thing of the past), or funeral directors (death will be eliminated). As I mentioned earlier, even my job as a preacher will probably be eliminated since there will be no sin to preach against and "the earth will be filled with the knowledge of the glory of the LORD" (Hab. 2:14).

This doesn't mean that people like myself will be unemployed and living on welfare. Perhaps for us what was merely a hobby on earth will become a vocation in heaven. Or maybe God will assign us a new task—one that we will be uniquely suited to perform. The majority of Christians should not be surprised that their work in the new heaven and new earth may very well be an extension and enhancement of their work now—minus the impediments that currently drain the joy out of that work.

From Cultivation to Creation

If life in the Garden of Eden serves as a template of what we can expect in heaven, then we can look forward to an eternity cultivating and creating. In the beginning, God created nature and called it good. But God intended His image-bearers to cultivate nature—to work it and create something very good.

For example, cherries are good, but cherry pie is very good; avocados are good, but guacamole is very good; tomatoes and spices are good, but salsa is very good. So when God created the man and placed him in the garden, He commissioned Adam to cultivate and keep what God had begun. But more than a cultivator, Adam was also to be a creator, which he demonstrated when he employed his imagination to name the animals.

The job descriptions of cultivator and creator are still in effect in today's world. The automobile, airplane, computer, and iPhone are examples of humankind's God-given creativity at work to make the world an even more enjoyable place in which to live.

We shouldn't be surprised that we will continue our creative work in the new heaven and new earth. Why wouldn't we bake cherry pies, eat salsa, write books, make movies, produce songs, teach classes, or do a thousand other things we do on earth?

If you want a clue about what your work might be in heaven, ask yourself the question my friend Bobb Biehl once posed to me: "If money and education were not a factor and you could do anything in the world with the guarantee you wouldn't fail, what would you do?" Why is that a relevant question? According to Philippians 2:13, "God . . . is at work within you, giving you the will and the power to achieve his purpose" (Phillips). God is the One who plants the "will" or desire in our hearts to accomplish His purpose for our lives. One of the best indicators of what we should be doing in this life and what we will be doing in the next life is based on desires God has placed in our hearts.

God doesn't waste gifts, experiences, or desires on us—they are all essential components of our unique purpose—not just in this life but in the life to come as well. Remember, our lives are each a continuum that begins on earth and extends beyond the grave. Who we are on earth is who we will be in heaven. We don't become someone else when we die—with different interests, gifts, skills, responsibilities, or callings. Therefore, we can assume that our work on the new earth will in some way resemble the work God has called us to perform on this present earth.

One Specific Job Description: Rule and Reign

Besides cultivating and creating, Adam and Eve were to rule and reign as God's coregents over creation—to be king and queen of earth.

> Then God said, "Let Us make man in Our image, according to Our likeness; and let them rule over the fish of the sea and over the birds of the sky and over the cattle and over all

the earth, and over every creeping thing that creeps on the earth." (Gen. 1:26; see v. 28)

But their conscious decision to rebel against God forced them to abdicate their reign over creation. In time, God sent a "second Adam"—Jesus Christ—and established a second Eve—the church—to one day rule over a new kingdom. And when Christ returns and establishes His thousand-year reign on earth (a period of time commonly referred to as the millennium), He will appoint His faithful followers (you and me) to rule with Him.

Christ's kingdom will not be run by professional politicians (do I hear an "Amen!"?) but by His followers. The criteria by which leaders in the new world order are selected will be completely different than in today's world. Cronyism and compromise will play no role in the selection of rulers. Instead, men and women will be elevated to leadership positions in the new world according to their faithfulness and service to God in the present world.

However, our reign will extend beyond the thousand-year rule of Christ during the millennium into the eternal state of the new heaven and new earth. The prophet Daniel had a vision of the coming Messiah—Jesus—and was told:

> The saints of the Highest One will receive the kingdom and possess the kingdom forever, for all ages to come. . . . [And] the sovereignty, the dominion and the greatness of all the kingdoms under the whole heaven will be given to the people of the saints of the Highest One; His kingdom will be an everlasting kingdom, and all the dominions will serve and obey Him. (Dan. 7:18, 27)

When this happens, we will fulfill on the new earth the role God originally assigned to Adam and Even on the old earth—we "will reign forever and ever" (Rev. 22:5).

Ruling and reigning with Christ sounds intriguing. But who is qualified to reign? What exactly does reigning entail? And what is the extent of our reign?

Who Gets to Rule and Reign?

I've heard countless preachers opine that those who will rule with Christ in the next world will be His lowliest followers in this world, those who perform the most menial jobs imaginable. The only requirement for being assigned a leadership role in the next world, these preachers claim, is having the right character qualities in this world—character traits outlined by Jesus in the Beatitudes: humility, purity, peacefulness, and mercy.

I couldn't disagree more. While character certainly counts with God in both this world and the next, character is not the only prerequisite for leadership. Those who will rule and reign with Christ in the new world will be those who have the *desire* and the *ability* to rule. Frankly, there are wonderfully dedicated Christians who are absolutely terrified at the prospect of having to be in charge of anything. For them, having vast leadership responsibilities for eternity would be more like hell than heaven.

If that's true of you, relax. If you enjoy working with your hands more than directing other people, chances are that is what you will be doing in the new world as well. If you are more comfortable working one-on-one with other people rather than casting a vision for thousands, don't be surprised if God places you in a similar role in the new heaven. Usually, the only people who get excited about ruling and reigning with Christ for eternity are those who enjoy leadership roles in this world.

However, just having the desire and skills necessary for leadership does not automatically qualify you to rule with Christ in the new world. The single greatest determiner of leadership responsibilities in the next life will be faithfulness to God in this life. As we've discussed before, what you do on earth echoes in the halls of heaven.

Jesus powerfully illustrated that truth in His parable of the minas recorded in Luke 19. The story—which is equally applicable to our role in the millennial kingdom and the eternal state—begins with a nobleman traveling to a "distant country to receive a kingdom" (Luke 19:12). This is a reference to Jesus's death, resurrection, and ascension to heaven, where He now rules at the right hand of God the Father.[8] When Christ returns to earth, as the nobleman returned from his journey, He will establish His kingdom—first during the millennium and then for eternity.[9]

However, before departing on his journey, the nobleman gave to each of his ten servants a single mina—a Greek coin worth one hundred drachmas, or about three months' wages. The mina represents the totality of the time, treasure, and opportunities God has granted to all of us in this life. Each one of us is given only one life to live and invest for the Lord before He returns. And just as the nobleman, upon his return, required his servants to account for their use of the minas, so Christ will one day require each of us to account for the lives He has entrusted to us.

In Jesus's story the first servant reported a 1,000 percent return on investment, earning the nobleman's praise. "Well done, good slave," he said to the first servant, "because you have been faithful in a very little thing, you are to be in authority over ten cities" (Luke 19:17). The second servant reported a 500 percent return and was given authority over "five cities" (v. 19).

But a third servant wasn't nearly as industrious. Instead of investing the money wisely, he hid the mina, fearing recrimination from his master if he lost the money through a poor investment. Instead of rewarding this servant, the nobleman condemned him. "Why did you not put my money in the bank, and [then] I would have collected it with interest?" the nobleman asked (v. 23).

His master had given this third servant one mina and he returned exactly one mina to his master. His mistake was failing to leverage what had been entrusted to him. Remember, the mina represents all that God has entrusted to us during our brief stay on earth. Everything we have—our time, our money, our gifts, our opportunities—is simply on loan to us from God to use to expand His kingdom.

But here's the paradox. Although our existence on earth is a "little thing" (v. 17) compared to eternity, we have the opportunity to leverage the value of our lives on earth by investing it in the expansion of God's kingdom. Our ability and willingness to make such an investment will determine our responsibilities in the new kingdom Christ establishes when He returns.

Unfortunately, the third slave failed to wisely invest what had been entrusted to him during his master's brief absence and received the nobleman's condemnation instead of commendation. And what had been given to the third servant was taken away and given to the first servant, because "to everyone who has, more shall be given, but from the one who does not have, even what he does have shall be taken away" (Luke 19:26).

God has placed within our hands not only a precious treasure—our life—but also a great responsibility: to use our limited time and treasure in this life to further God's agenda rather than our own.

What Does Ruling and Reigning Look Like?

Ruling and reigning with Christ in His new kingdom involves at least two responsibilities: judging and governing. In 1 Corinthians 6:2, Paul wrote: "the saints will judge the world." The Greek word translated "judge" (*krino*) can refer to pronouncing a verdict against someone or it can be a synonym for governing. As corulers with Jesus Christ we will be responsible for both judging and governing in His new kingdom. Although there is no indication in Scripture that you and I will pronounce judgments against other human beings, we very well could be involved in the future judgment of certain angels.

In 1 Corinthians 6:3, Paul asked: "Do you not know that we will judge angels?" This is a curious question, since Psalm 8:4–5 says God made humans lower than angels. But in the eternal state, our positions are reversed—we'll be elevated higher than angels. Perhaps Paul was referring to the fallen angels who are awaiting judgment for their sin of cohabiting with women as described in Genesis 6. Or Paul may have used "judge" as a synonym for our responsibility of ruling over the angelic orders in the new heaven and new earth. We'll have to wait for heaven to find the answer to this question.

I believe that those who rule with Christ during the millennium and in the new heaven and new earth will be primarily involved in governing God's vast kingdom. It was an ancient practice for kings to appoint faithful citizens to serve as coregents over all or portions of the king's kingdom. At least three men in the Old Testament were appointed as prime minister over their respective nations: Joseph over Egypt (Gen. 41:38–44), Daniel over Babylon and the Medo-Persian Empire (Dan. 6:3), and Mordecai over Persia (Esther 8:1–2; 10:3). Although Scripture provides few details about what ruling in God's new kingdom will entail, we can be confident the experience will be exhilarating and eternally fulfilling since it is a reward for faithfulness to God in this life.

God assigned Adam and Eve to reign over the Lord's old creation. In the same way, those who are rewarded with leadership responsibilities will be assigned to reign over the Lord's new creation—the new heavens and the new earth. That leadership will include the governing of Christians who will work in Christ's glorious new kingdom. And though our primary residence will be the New Jerusalem, our work will take us beyond the new earth and into the far-flung galaxies of the new heavens—the stellar space, with its innumerable stars and planets.

Three Permanent Perks of Heaven

Don't think that heaven will be all work and no fun. Even though performing fulfilling work is one thing we will do in heaven, it is not the *only* thing we will do. Beyond worshiping

God and working for God, the Bible indicates at least three other activities that will occupy our time in the new heaven and the new earth.

Enjoying Other Believers

We were made to live in community—and that need for other people will not disappear in eternity. But in the new heaven and new earth, we'll experience the most intimate and fulfilling relationships imaginable. My friend David Jeremiah observes:

> Because we will be God's people made over, we will be perfectly compatible with one another and able, for the first time ever, to enjoy the intimate fellowship that we all long for in our hearts.[10]

Gone will be the suspicion, impure motives, and selfishness that taint even the best relationships we experience now. We will enjoy perfect fellowship not only with those we already know but also with those heroes of our faith we have only read about.

Just imagine how fascinating it will be to talk with Adam about what life was like in the Garden before sin entered the world. We will sit riveted to stories of

- Noah and his experience during the Great Flood,
- God's last-minute intervention in Abraham's offering of Isaac,
- the children of Israel escaping Pharaoh's chariots,
- David's victory over the giant Goliath, and

- the surprising discovery of Jesus's followers on that first Easter Sunday morning.

We will talk theology with Augustine, Jerome, Martin Luther, and John Calvin; science with Blaise Pascal, Isaac Newton, and George Washington Carver. We will discuss courage with William Wilberforce and Martin Luther King Jr., or what it was like to compose Christianity's most beloved hymn with John Newton. We will review books with G. K. Chesterton, J. R. R. Tolkien, and C. S. Lewis. And we will learn what it was like to preach before thousands from Dwight L. Moody and Billy Graham.

From our first day in heaven, and for every day thereafter, we will walk the streets of the new heaven and new earth with astonishment: "There goes Jeremiah! And over there is Eve. I can't believe it—there's Paul talking with the Wesley brothers—John and Charles. And over there is Esther . . . and Caleb . . . and John . . . and . . . Solomon . . . and . . ."

Better bring your autograph book with you—it's going to be quite an experience.

Learning More about God

As we saw earlier, the prophet Habakkuk promised that a day was coming when "the earth will be filled with the knowledge of the glory of the LORD" (Hab. 2:14). Perhaps Paul had this verse in mind when he wrote to the Corinthians: "Now I know in part, but then I will know fully just as I also have been fully known" (1 Cor. 13:12).

In the new heaven and new earth we will certainly understand more about God than we do now. But exactly how

117

will that knowledge come? At the moment of our death and entrance into the presence of God, will the Lord instantaneously download into our minds a perfect and complete understanding of Himself? Maybe.

But think about your most valued relationships on earth—your mate, your children, your closest friends. No doubt you've discovered the joy of learning more about them through the years rather than experiencing an information dump all at once. Imagine how boring eternity would be if we knew everything there is to know about God and had nothing new to discover for eternity.

I can just hear some seasoned student of Scripture shouting, "But what about Jeremiah 31:34? 'They will not teach again, each man his neighbor and each man his brother, saying, "Know the LORD," for they will all know Me, from the least of them to the greatest of them.' Doesn't that verse imply an instantaneous and complete understanding of God?"

The kind of teaching Jeremiah says will no longer be needed in God's kingdom is an exhortation to enter into a relationship with God. That's what he meant by "know the LORD." Everyone in the new heaven and new earth will already have a relationship with God. But that doesn't mean everyone will immediately and instantaneously know everything there is to know about God.

For example, when I first met my wife, Amy, in Mrs. Denny's seventh-grade math class, I knew nothing about her except that she was the prettiest girl I had ever seen! But as we began passing notes back and forth (and always getting into trouble for doing so) I learned more about her. Over time, that friendship blossomed into romance, leading to an engagement and eventually forty years of marriage. And with every year that passes I continue to learn new things about her.

If I can continue to learn new things about a finite human being like Amy, how much more is there to learn about our infinite God? As one theologian put it:

> We will constantly be more amazed with God, more in love with God, and thus ever more relishing his presence and our relationship with him. Our experience of God will never reach its consummation. We will never finally arrive, as if upon reaching a peak we discover there is nothing beyond. Our experience of God will never become stale. It will deepen and develop, intensify and amplify, unfold and increase, broaden and balloon.[11]

Experiencing Real Rest

We've already seen that in eternity we will not be consigned to floating on a cloud plucking a harp. God has a very real assignment for each of us—work that will exhilarate us and free us from the earthly encumbrances that exhaust us. This doesn't mean, however, that we will not rest. When God created the world He rested on the seventh day—not because He was exhausted but in order to reflect on what He had accomplished. And He set aside days, weeks, and years for the nation of Israel to rest.

God understands that we live under the tyranny of the urgent, which induces stress. This is why Jesus said to the exhausted and wrung-out: "Come to Me, all who are weary and heavy-laden, and I will give you rest" (Matt. 11:28). That promise transcends this old earth and carries forward to the

119

new earth. In Revelation 14:13, the apostle John was commanded to write these words: "Blessed are the dead who die in the Lord from now on . . . that they may rest from their labors, for their deeds follow with them."

The promise given to John refers to those believers who will be martyred for their faith during the great tribulation. They will finally experience relief from their labors. John did not mean that they will never have to work again or that they will enter into an eternal nap. The Greek word *kopos*, translated "labors," means that these believers, along with future believers, will be released from the tiresome burden of trying to live a godly life in a godless world.

But the kind of rest we will enjoy in the new heaven and the new earth goes far beyond the absence of hostility and persecution. The rest Jesus promised actually has nothing to do with imperfect bodies that tire quickly because of sin's curse. The rest Jesus is referring to will be the same kind of rest our heavenly Father experienced after six days of creating the universe.

It is a momentary respite from work that allows us to savor the satisfaction of a job well done.

It is a cessation from labor that allows us to reflect upon what we have accomplished and to say, "It is good . . . it is very good!"

It is a rest that reminds us that as important as our work will be—even in the new heaven and new earth—there will be other aspects of life to be enjoyed as well, not least of which include the perfect relationships with others and with God we have always longed for.

6

Do People in Heaven Know
What Is Happening on Earth?

For behold, I create new heavens and a new earth;
And the former things will not be remembered or come to
mind.

Isaiah 65:17

Imagine you're dead. You're standing at the entrance to
heaven. Peter is there to greet you. He takes your name and
checks your reservation. Everything is in order so he welcomes you into heaven with a smile. As he escorts you to
your room, he hands you a package: a white robe, a golden
crown, and a theater ticket.

The robe and crown aren't necessarily a surprise—you
remember reading something, somewhere, about heavenly
robes and crowns. But a ticket—that is unexpected. "What's
the ticket for?" you ask. "Oh, that's for the movie," Peter

answers. "Tonight we're having a double feature. The first stars your friend, the one who died with you in the car accident. It's a tragedy . . . really, 'horror film' is perhaps a better description, because your friend didn't make it here. He's in hell. However, the second movie is about your life. It stars you, with a supporting cast that includes your mate, your children, and dozens of friends and acquaintances. The climactic scene is your funeral. It's a real tearjerker. But I don't want to spoil it for you. I think you'll really enjoy the show!"

Before you have a chance to respond, Peter says, "Ah, here we are. Here's your key. Get some rest. And be sure to get to the theater early. It's going to be a sellout. All of heaven will be in attendance." With that, Peter smiles, turns in his sandals, and walks away.

I'm pretty sure there aren't tickets given out in heaven to movies depicting your life. Or movies starring those who enter hell. But many people do wonder whether residents of heaven can watch what is taking place on earth, or even peer into the darkness of hell. And if they do, could they be watching you right now?

Heaven's Witnesses

After guiding us on a tour through the hall of heroes in Hebrews 11, the author concludes:

> Therefore, since we have so great a cloud of witnesses surrounding us, let us also lay aside every encumbrance and the sin which so easily entangles us, and let us run with endurance the race that is set before us. (Heb. 12:1)

At first glance, this verse appears to imply that the current occupants of heaven are like spectators at a track meet, sitting in the stands watching the occupants of earth run the race of faith.

If we're honest, there's something a little creepy about the thought of a billion eyes watching your every move. To think that Solomon—the author of the manual on marital love that bears his name—might have a peephole into your bedroom might be a little disconcerting. Or what about your grandmother watching you as you . . . well, you get the idea!

But is that what Hebrews 12:1 teaches? Although the word "witnesses" does imply spectators, the verse doesn't really teach that all of heaven's population is sitting around watching us while munching on popcorn and slurping Coke. In the context, the "cloud of witnesses" refers only to those Old Testament saints mentioned in Hebrews 11. The point the writer is making is that in light of the example of those who persevered in their faith, we should also keep moving forward in obeying God regardless of the obstacles we face.

Nevertheless, there is some indication that those in heaven are aware of what takes place outside of heaven. For example, Christ must be aware of the obedience and disobedience of Christians on earth, since He condemned and commended the seven churches in Revelation 2–3. Furthermore, the apostle Paul realized that a heavenly audience was witnessing his actions on earth since he described his life as "a spectacle to the world, both to angels and to men" (1 Cor. 4:9). We can assume from this verse that angels are also aware of the activities of people on earth.

But Scripture provides us with other examples of those in heaven who seem to know what is happening on earth.

Abraham and the Rich Man

We have already dealt with Jesus's story in Luke 16 of Lazarus and the rich man in chapter 4. But there is one more observation we need to make from this story. Once the rich man arrived in hades—the temporary residence of the un-saved dead—he was immediately aware of his own agony and Lazarus's joy in heaven. This is important because some theologians and Christian traditions (like Seventh-Day Adventists) teach that consciousness ceases to exist at death—an idea sometimes called "soul sleep."[1]

The rich man addressed Abraham, and Abraham answered the rich man—indicating that both were fully conscious. Both men thought, spoke, heard, saw, felt, remembered, and recognized each other. And both men knew what was happening in each other's world. The rich man knew of Lazarus's pleasure, while Abraham knew of the rich man's anguish.

It appears the occupants of hades are aware of what is taking place in heaven, and the occupants of heaven are aware of what is taking place in hades. But do people in heaven know what is taking place on earth?

The Tribulation Martyrs and the Judgment on Earth

During that terrible future time of God's judgment on the earth known as the tribulation—the seven years between the rapture of the church and the second coming of Christ—many will come to faith in Jesus. However, just as Christians in the Middle East today are being slaughtered for their faith, future "tribulation saints" will also be required to pay the ultimate price for following Christ. When John had his heavenly vision, he saw these martyred believers gathered around God's throne, crying out for justice against those who had murdered them.

> When the Lamb broke the fifth seal, I saw underneath the altar the souls of those who had been slain because of the word of God, and because of the testimony which they had maintained; and they cried out with a loud voice, saying, "How long, O Lord, holy and true, will You refrain from judging and avenging our blood on those who dwell on the earth?" (Rev. 6:9–10)

These slain Christ-followers in heaven were acutely aware of what was happening—or not happening—on the earth. Their persecutors on earth were continuing their assault against God's people without restraint. Their cry was, "God, how long are you going to allow these enemies of Christ to continue? It's time to step in and do something!" Obviously, their frustration over God's (seeming) inaction was only possible because of their awareness of what was taking place on earth.

Later in John's vision, at the end of the tribulation and before the climactic battle of Armageddon, all the saints of heaven rose up with a great roar of approval over God's judgment on earth. These saints shouted:

> Hallelujah! Salvation and glory and power belong to our God; because His judgments are true and righteous; for He has judged the great harlot [Babylon] who was corrupting the earth with her immorality, and He has avenged the blood of His bond-servants on her. (19:1–2)

Again, the praise of believers in heaven for God's judgment against His enemies on the earth will only be possible if indeed the residents of heaven are aware of what is happening on earth.

Heaven's Saints and the Salvation of the Unsaved

Jesus loved to tell stories. Three of His most famous are in Luke 15: the parables of the lost sheep, the lost coin, and the lost son. All three of these stories share the same purpose: to contrast the attitude of the self-righteous Pharisees, who hated sinners, with the attitude of the truly righteous God, who *loves* sinners. Jesus's point in all three parables was the same: when you lose something of value—a sheep, a coin, a child—you don't curse the lost object. Instead, you search for it and celebrate when you've found it.

God has the same attitude toward people who are living apart from Him. God doesn't hate those who are "lost." He loves them and is overjoyed when He is reunited with them. But Jesus said that God is not the only One who is ecstatic when a sinner is reunited with God:

> I tell you . . . there will be more joy *in heaven* over one sinner who repents than over ninety-nine righteous persons who need no repentance. . . . [And] there is joy *in the presence of the angels* of God over one sinner who repents. (Luke 15:7, 10)

Jesus didn't say angels rejoiced over repentant lost sinners—though they probably do. Jesus said rejoicing took place "in heaven . . . in the *presence* of the angels," indicating that Christians in heaven are celebrating the salvation of sinners on earth. Think about this: besides God, who in heaven would appreciate the salvation of a non-Christian (especially if that non-Christian happened to be a friend or family member) more than those who had already experienced redemption?

If citizens of heaven rejoice at the salvation of sinners, then they not only know what is taking place on earth in a general sense but they are aware of the specific choices individuals are making on earth—whether they have accepted or rejected Christ's offer of salvation.

Hell's Captives

Since it appears that believers in heaven are aware of the faith commitments of those on earth, will those same heavenly believers lament the damnation of others? And if so, how could anyone ever be happy in heaven, knowing that people they cared about on earth are being tormented forever in hell?

These are intriguing questions. But before I address them there are some truths about hell we need to understand.

The Necessity of Hell

Hell was not part of God's original creation—it wasn't necessary. When God created the universe He called it "good." In fact, it was "very good." But when Satan rebelled and enlisted the first couple in his coup against the Almighty, hell became a necessity. Author Warren Wiersbe explains why:

Hell is a witness to the righteous character of God. He must judge sin. Hell is also a witness to man's responsibility, the fact that he is not a robot or a helpless victim, but a creature able to make choices. God does not "send people to hell"; they send themselves by rejecting the Savior. . . . Hell is also a witness to the awfulness of sin. If we once saw sin as God sees it, we would understand why a place such as hell exists.[2]

Satan's purpose in the world is both sinister and simple: use every means available to undermine and destroy God's plan for His universe. And because every human being since the fall of the first couple has been infected with the sin virus, Satan has millions of willing accomplices to aid him in his efforts.

When people ask the question, "Why does God allow evil in the world?" they need look no further than the mirror! Human beings, not God, are responsible for the terrible conditions of our planet.

Why do our cities suffer with prostitution, gang warfare, and drug abuse?

Why do our corporations and governments struggle with lying, cover-ups, and corruption?

Why are families being destroyed by divorce, adultery, and pornography?

Why do churches split over issues such as worship style, pastoral personalities, and the pressure to be culturally relevant?

These are just some of the devastating consequences of rebelling against our Creator. But this rebellion will not last forever. One day the universe will be restored to its original state. Evil will no longer triumph—or even exist. But for that to happen, those who have refused God's love will have to be quarantined from believers in the afterlife. If unbelievers were not isolated in hell from the rest of creation, then evil would once again infect God's creation and destroy the new heaven and the new earth.

What Do We Mean by "Hell"?

As we saw in chapter 4, the Greek word *hades* refers to the temporary location of the unsaved dead. The New Testament uses two other Greek words to describe the destination of the unsaved we commonly refer to as "hell."

The apostle Peter used the word *tartaros* when he said, "God did not spare angels when they sinned, but cast them into hell [*tartaros*] and committed them to pits of darkness, reserved for judgment" (2 Pet. 2:4). Just as hades is a temporary destination for unsaved people, *tartaros* is a temporary prison for a certain group of wicked angels.

Most demons (angels who chose to follow Satan in his original rebellion against God) are free to roam the earth, engaging in destructive activities whenever they find opportunity. But the imprisoned demons in *tartaros* are not free to roam because they committed a particularly heinous sin against God. Many believe this sin was their cohabitation with women on earth as described in Genesis 6—a sin that caused God to immediately dispatch them to this holding place of *tartaros* until their final judgment:

> And angels who did not keep their own domain, but abandoned their proper abode, [God] has kept in eternal bonds under darkness for the judgment of the great day. (Jude 6)

That "great day" of judgment will be when God throws Satan and all his fallen angels into "the lake of fire and brimstone" (Rev. 20:10). The Greek word *gehenna*, which is also translated as "hell" in English Bibles, refers to this place of eternal torment for Satan and his demons, the Antichrist and false prophet, and all unbelievers. The name is derived from the Hebrew *gen hinnom*—"the valley of Hinnom" or "the valley of Ben Hinnom."[3] Eventually, the name was shortened to *ge-hinnom* and the Greek translation became *gehenna*.

The valley of Hinnom is located immediately southwest of Jerusalem. During Jeremiah's day, the valley was the place where Jews offered human sacrifices, including burning children alive to the false god Molech.[4] Jeremiah called the place "the valley of the Slaughter" (Jer. 7:30–33).

By the time of Christ, the valley had become Jerusalem's city dump and a burial ground for criminals. Because of the valley's sordid history with child sacrifices, Jews in the first century associated *gehenna* with the place of eternal damnation and punishment for the wicked. According to Jesus, *gehenna* was the place of "outer darkness; [the] place [of] weeping and gnashing of teeth . . . where their worm does not die, and the fire is not quenched" (Matt. 8:12; Mark 9:48). This is the eternal destination of everyone who refuses to trust in Jesus Christ for the forgiveness of sins.

What Is Hell Like?

In *The Screwtape Letters*, C. S. Lewis puts into the mouth of hell's chief demon these words: "Indeed the safest road to hell is the gradual one—the gentle slope, soft underfoot, without sudden turnings, without milestones, without signposts."[5] No doubt that is true. Jesus said the way to hell is broad and its gate is wide (Matt. 7:13). It's easy to get into hell but impossible to leave it. What does the Bible reveal about this very real destination for those who die without Christ?

As we piece together what the Bible says about hades (the immediate but temporary destination of the unsaved) and *gehenna* (the eternal destination of the unsaved, also known as "the lake of fire" or "hell"), we can discover some important information about this terrible place. For simplicity, from this point on we will use the general term "hell" to describe both the temporary and eternal destination of the unsaved.

HELL IS A PHYSICAL LOCATION

Like heaven, hell has an address. In the story of the rich man and Lazarus, hell is described as being "far away" (Luke 16:23), consisting of flames (v. 24), and being separated from heaven by "a great chasm fixed" (v. 26). These phrases describe an actual location, not a state of mind. And John described hell as "the lake of fire" (Rev. 19:20; 20:10, 14–15). At the end of the final judgment, before the unveiling of the new heaven and new earth, John observed, "death and Hades were thrown into the lake of fire" (20:14). Only a physical place (hades) can be thrown into another physical place (the lake of fire).

Jesus's words in Matthew 25:32–46 about the separation of the sheep and goats strongly argue for the fact that hell is a geographical location. At the end of the seven years of tribulation Jesus will separate believers (sheep) from unbelievers (goats). He said the goats will "go away into eternal punishment" (hell), while the sheep will go "into eternal life" (heaven) (v. 46). It is simply illogical for Jesus to say that believers go to an actual location (heaven) while unbelievers are dispatched to an unpleasant state of mind (hell). Elsewhere in Matthew 25 Jesus leaves no doubt about the reality of hell when He describes unbelievers as being "accursed" and cast "into the eternal fire which has been prepared for the devil and his angels" (v. 41).

Though hell and its flames are real, the fires of hell will not consume the bodies or spirits of those thrown into them. Rather, these unbelievers will suffer physical and spiritual anguish for all eternity. Like burning your hand on a hot stove without scorching your flesh, those in hell will experience the sensation without the scars.

Hell Is a Place of Eternal, Physical Torment

The Bible teaches that the bodies of everyone who has ever lived—Christians and non-Christians alike—will experience a "resurrection." Christians will receive a new body that will allow them to enjoy the indescribable pleasures of the new heaven and new earth. Unbelievers will receive a body that will allow them to experience the real and eternal suffering of hell.

If you have difficulty believing that God would give non-Christians a "new" body for the sole purpose of experiencing everlasting suffering, read carefully Jesus's words in John 5:

> Do not marvel at this; for an hour is coming, in which all who are in the tombs will hear [the Son of God's] voice, and will come forth; those who did the good deeds to a resurrection

of life, those who committed the evil deeds to a resurrection of judgment. (vv. 28–29)

John "saw" this future resurrection of the unsaved in his vision recorded in Revelation 20:11–15:

Then I saw a great white throne and Him who sat upon it, from whose presence earth and heaven fled away, and no place was found for them. And I saw the dead, the great and the small, standing before the throne, and books were opened; and another book was opened, which is the book of life; and the dead were judged from the things which were written in the books, according to their deeds. And the sea gave up the dead which were in it, and death and Hades gave up the dead which were in them; and they were judged, every one of them according to their deeds. Then death and Hades were thrown into the lake of fire. This is the second death, the lake of fire. And if anyone's name was not found written in the book of life, he was thrown into the lake of fire.

Some theologians have attempted to rescue God from the charge of cruel and unusual punishment by advancing the doctrine of annihilation. This belief theorizes that unbelievers are destroyed—or annihilated—instead of physically punished for eternity. One of the arguments proponents of annihilationism use is the fact that Jesus and Paul speak of the "destruction" of those who go to hell.[6] But the Greek word translated "destruction" (*olethros*) doesn't mean annihilation. It means "sudden ruin." It refers to separation from God and the loss of everything that makes life worth living.

As a pastor I frequently witness such destruction. For example, when a man destroys his family through adultery and divorce, or when an alcoholic destroys his reputation and dignity through addiction, the suffering they experience is not momentary but continues as long as they live.

The doctrine of annihilation also contradicts the clear teaching of Revelation 19:20 and 20:10. After the climactic battle of Armageddon and return of Jesus Christ to the earth, the Antichrist and the false prophet are thrown into the eternal "lake of fire" (Rev. 19:20). After a thousand years, Satan and his minions are also cast into this same lake of fire:

> The devil who deceived them was thrown into the lake of fire and brimstone, where the beast [the Antichrist] and the false prophet are also; and they will be tormented day and night forever and ever. (20:10)

Notice the phrase "where the beast and the false prophet *are*." If the Antichrist and the false prophet—both human beings—had been destroyed the moment they were cast into the lake of fire, John would have written: "where the beast and the false prophet *were*." But after one thousand years, these two are still alive and suffering in this place where "they will be tormented day and night forever and ever."

The phrase "forever and ever" is important because it re-iterates Jesus's claim that hell is a place of "eternal [physical] punishment" (Matt. 25:46). It's also important because it is the exact same phrase used by John to describe our endless worship of God, the endless life of God, and the endless kingdom of God.[7] My predecessor at First Baptist Church Dallas, Dr. W. A. Criswell, used to observe that if you reduce by one minute the time unbelievers have in hell then you must logically subtract the same amount of time believers will have in heaven, since the phrase "forever and ever" is used to describe the experience of believers and unbelievers alike.

HELL IS A PLACE OF INDESCRIBABLE LONELINESS

Many people joke that they'd rather go to hell than go to heaven because hell will be "party central." But there will be no parties in hell. No one will socialize in hell because no one will be able to see anyone or anything. Jesus described hell as a place of "outer darkness" (Matt. 8:12). It's a place without the light of Christ because everyone in hell will be "away from the presence of the Lord" (2 Thess. 1:9).

A friend of mine likes to explore caves. Many caves, like Carlsbad Caverns in New Mexico, are lit to accentuate stalagmites, stalactites, and other unusual rock formations. But on one of my friend's tours in a cave in Colorado, there was no light—except the light of flashlights or headlamps. Crawling on his belly over the muddy floor of the cave and squeezing himself through small holes, my friend was having the time of his life. However, when the guide told everyone to turn off their lights, the blackness of the cave enveloped him. He described the darkness as claustrophobic. Not only could he not see his hand in front of his face but he wasn't even sure whether his eyes were open or closed. He lost all sense of direction. And if it wasn't for his feet firmly planted on the floor of the cave, he couldn't have told you which way was up or down. There wasn't a speck of light anywhere. And though he knew people were around him—his wife, the guide, and other tourists—he had never felt so cut off from humanity in all his life. It was, he said, a darkness and isolation that cannot be explained or comprehended—only experienced.

That is something of what hell must be like for those who enter there—an abyss of utter darkness and loneliness.

HELL IS A PLACE OF NO RETURN

Hell is a forever destination. This was the point of the parable of Lazarus and the rich man. Abraham told the rich man, who was suffering temporary agony, that "a great chasm fixed" separated heaven from hades, "so that those who wish to come over from here [heaven] to you will not be able, and that none may cross over from there [hades] to us" (Luke 16:26). Once we die our eternal destinies are just that—eternal.

Novelist James Joyce, in *A Portrait of the Artist as a Young Man*, captures a hint of the hopelessness and despair all in hell must know. After describing for his congregation the suffering that takes place in hell, a preacher said:

> Consider finally that the torment of this infernal prison is increased by the company of the damned themselves. . . . In hell all laws are overturned—there is no thought of family or country, of ties, of relationships. The damned howl and scream at one another, their torture and rage intensified by the presence of beings tortured and raging like themselves. All sense of humanity is forgotten. The yells of the suffering sinners fill the remotest corners of the vast abyss. The mouths of the damned are full of blasphemies against God and of hatred for their fellow sufferers and of curses against those souls which were their accomplices in sin. . . . They turn upon those accomplices and upbraid them and curse them. But they are helpless and hopeless: it is too late now for repentance.[8]

No one escapes the confines of hell. Hell is a forever destination. If you wait until you enter the gates of hell to repent, you will have waited too long.

HELL WILL BE THE DESTINY OF THE MAJORITY OF HUMANITY

Many people believe there ought to be a hell for truly evil people—the Adolph Hitlers, Joseph Stalins, Pol Pots, Charles Mansons, and Osama bin Ladens of the world. But those same people find it inconceivable that many good people who've simply not trusted in Jesus for forgiveness would also be sentenced to a place of eternal torment. What about all those who've never heard the name of Jesus? Or those who have sincerely embraced other religions and are living moral, upright lives? Would God really consign them to such a horrendous place?

As I discuss in my book *Not All Roads Lead to Heaven*, Jesus taught that only a small percentage of the earth's population will ever discover the true path to eternal life. In Matthew 7:13–14, Jesus said:

> Enter through the narrow gate; for the gate is wide and the way is broad that leads to destruction, and there are *many* who enter through it. For the gate is small and the way is narrow that leads to life, and there are *few* who find it.

As difficult as it may be to accept, the "many" on the wide road are not just mass murderers, child rapists, and terrorists. Sincere, religious people who make good neighbors and love their children are also on the "highway to hell." Even people who claim they have performed religious works in the name of Jesus will be cast into hell by Jesus on the judgment day, as Jesus Himself revealed:

> Not everyone who says to Me, "Lord, Lord," will enter the kingdom of heaven, but he who does the will of My Father who is in heaven will enter. Many will say to Me on that day [of judgment], "Lord, Lord, did we not prophesy in Your name, and in Your name cast out demons, and in Your name perform many miracles?" And then I will declare to them, "I never knew you; depart from Me, you who practice lawlessness." (Matt. 7:21–23)

We struggle with Jesus's claim that the majority of people will be in hell because of our *low estimation of God*. We assume that God should be as tolerant of sin as we are. After all, we regularly overlook sin in others and ourselves, so why can't God? However, our tolerance of sin is not evidence of our godliness but of our godlessness.

Listen to God's scathing indictment of the Israelites—and all of us—in Psalm 50:21: "You thought that I was just like you." God isn't anything like us. His "eyes are too pure to approve evil" and He will not "look on wickedness with favor" (Hab. 1:13). And for that reason, He must and will punish sin. Every sinner has an opportunity to receive Christ's offer of forgiveness. To do so means heaven. And every sinner has an opportunity to reject Christ's offer of forgiveness. To do so means hell.

We also struggle with Jesus's words in Matthew 7 because we have *too high an estimation of ourselves*. Our own inflated sense of goodness and justice causes us to set ourselves up as the measure of all goodness and justice. And by that measure, especially compared with the Hitlers or bin Ladens of the world, we measure up quite nicely . . . or so we think.

But God utilizes a different standard of moral measurement than ours. For example, the difference between the North Pole and the South Pole is negligible compared to the distance between the North Pole and the furthest star in the universe. In the same way, the moral difference between Adolph Hitler and us is substantial, but it's minimal compared to the difference between a perfect God and an imperfect humanity.

God's standard is perfect holiness. None of us meets that standard. And because we don't, Paul wrote: "For all have sinned and fall short of the glory of God" (Rom. 3:23). Unbelievers will spend eternity in hell, not because they're not good but because they're not *good enough*. In this, Christian philosopher Peter Kreeft was correct: "Hell is not populated mainly by passionate rebels but by nice, bland, indifferent, respectable people who simply never gave a damn [about Jesus Christ]."[9]

Will the Joy of Heaven Be Diminished by What Happens on Earth and in Hell?

It seems clear that believers in heaven know what is taking place on earth—at least in some sense. And they know what is taking place in hell according to the story of Lazarus and the rich man. So a natural question is how can we be happy in heaven while watching those we care about on earth suffering from devastating illnesses, broken relationships, or destructive addictions?

And how could we ever enjoy one pleasure of the new heaven and new earth knowing that some of those friends and family members we love the most will be suffering in hell? To put a finer point on it: Could you really enjoy all that God has prepared for you—no matter how spectacular—knowing that one of your children is being tormented day and night forever and ever?

This is a difficult question to answer because we lack the wisdom and insight to fully understand the mind of God. However, here are three possible answers to the question of how we can reconcile our joy in heaven with our knowledge of the suffering of our loved ones on earth and in hell.

Will God Purge Our Memories?

One Christian thinker frames the theory this way: "God may erase memories for a wayward son from the mind of his mother so that she may enjoy the full bliss of heaven unaware that she even had the son who is now damned."[10] This idea comes from Isaiah 65:17:

> For behold, I create new heavens and a new earth;
> And *the former things will not be remembered or*
> *come to mind.*

However, this can't mean that we'll forget *everything* about our former lives on earth. Many of the relationships we formed here will continue there—including our relationship with Christ. For example, Scripture says Jesus retains His scars (John 20:24–29). Seeing them will be a constant reminder that our sin compelled Him to endure the cross.

And the reminder of our sin that necessitated His death will compel us to enthusiastically worship Him for eternity.

The context of Isaiah 65:17 is verse 16. Speaking to the nation of Israel, the Lord said, "the former troubles are forgotten . . . they are hidden from My sight!" It is God who does the "forgetting," not us. This doesn't mean our omniscient God can't recall Israel's past transgressions. Rather, God *chooses* not to hold Israel's sin against her. When I forgive someone that doesn't mean I do a "memory wipe" of the wrong he or she committed against me. Even if I wanted to forget the offense, it would be biologically impossible to do so, since every experience we have is chemically and electrically embedded in our brain. Instead, forgiveness means letting go of my right to hurt another person for hurting me.

Nothing in Scripture indicates that God is going to erase our memories of those we know and love who may be suffering on earth or in hell.

Christians Will Be Preoccupied with the Joys of Heaven

We are all aware of the multitude of starving children, disease-ridden acquaintances and loved ones, and persecuted Christians in the world around us. Yet the knowledge of these suffering individuals does not prevent us from enjoying a good meal, a day at the beach, or time with our family. Some would claim that our ability to enjoy these blessings, in spite of others' suffering, is a testimony to our selfishness. "In heaven, we will be like Jesus, who wept over the fate of the lost," they argue.

While it is true that Jesus cried over the eternal destiny of the residents of Jerusalem while He was on earth, there is no indication that Jesus will do any crying in heaven. The writer of Hebrews notes that Jesus willingly "endured the cross" so that He could experience "the joy set before Him" when He "sat down at the right hand of the throne of God" (Heb. 12:2).

Additionally, Scripture teaches that complete joy will be the primary emotion of those in heaven:

> You will make known to me the path of life;
> In Your presence is *fullness of joy*;
> In Your right hand there are pleasures forever.
>   (Ps. 16:11)

In heaven we *will* be just like Jesus, who experiences the "fullness of joy" in spite of all that is happening on earth and in hell.

We Will Understand the Plan and Justice of God

In his book *The Eighth Day*, Thornton Wilder compares our lives to a tapestry. Viewed from the right side—the side facing out—we see an intricate work of art made from thousands of multicolored threads woven together to form a beautiful picture. But if we look at the backside of the tapestry, we see a jumble of threads of varying lengths crisscrossing one another. Nothing seems to make sense. Some threads are knotted, others are short, and still others are long.

The point Wilder is making is simple: God has a design for our lives. Some lives are twisted, knotted, or cut short. Other lives are of impressive length and color. Why? Not because one thread is more important than another thread, but because God's tapestry requires it.

Only from the perspective of heaven will we be able to see the right side of God's plan for our lives and understand how He is working all things "together for good" (Rom. 8:28). The tangled mess of broken relationships, catastrophic accidents, and sudden deaths that make no sense to those of us trapped in time and space on earth will be viewed completely differently from the perspective of heaven—even as we witness those tragedies being experienced by those we care about most.

But what about those we love who will be condemned to eternal torment in hell? It's important to note that God *doesn't* send people to hell; they freely *choose* to go to hell by rejecting God's gift of salvation through Jesus's death and resurrection. "God's wrath . . . is something which men choose for themselves," theologian J. I. Packer wrote. "Before hell is an experience inflicted by God, it is a state for which man himself opts, by retreating from the light which God shines in his heart to lead him to Himself."[11]

As difficult as this truth is to accept on this side of heaven—especially when talking about loved ones—the people in hell are there because they deserve it. But on the other side of heaven, we'll see God's justice in punishing those who refused to accept Christ's sacrifice as perfect, holy, and just. The apostle Paul claims that when we see Jesus Christ "dealing out retribution to those who do not know God and to those who do not obey the gospel of our Lord Jesus" (2 Thess. 1:8), none of us will accuse Jesus of injustice. Instead, Jesus Christ the Judge will "be marveled at among all who have believed" (v. 10).

Although this truth is hard to fathom, Packer offers some helpful words:

Remember, in heaven our minds, hearts, motives, and feelings will be sanctified, so that we are fully conformed to the character and outlook of Jesus our Lord. . . . In heaven, glorifying God and thanking him for everything will always absorb us. All our love for and joy in others who are with us in heaven will spring from their doing the same, and love and pity of hell's occupants will not enter our hearts. Their hell will not veto our heaven.[12]

And we can add with certainty that our awareness of anything happening on earth or in hell is incapable of diminishing the fullness of our joy in that place called heaven.

7

Will We Know
One Another in Heaven?

Dear friends, we are already God's children, but he has not
yet shown us what we will be like when Christ appears. But
we do know that we will be like him, for we will see him as
he really is.

1 John 3:2 NLT

Growing old isn't for the faint of heart—especially for those
with a faint heart. With age come ailments and aches . . .
and a few extra pounds. As humor columnist Erma Bombeck grew older she said something along the lines of,
"I'm not telling you what I weigh, but when I measure my
girth and then step on the scales, I oughta be a ninety-foot
redwood."[1]

For many of us the battle of the bulge was a minor skir-
mish in our twenties. But it became total war in our forties

and fifties. And if it wasn't the bulge, it was something else—wrinkles or sags or bags.

Have you ever gotten out of the shower and stared at yourself in a full-length mirror? For those of us of a certain age, it's unnerving. You ought to try it sometime; it'll jolt you awake—like an electric shock. One overriding thought will fill your mind: *I have everything I used to have. It's just a few inches lower than where it used to be.* Let's not kid ourselves: our bodies aren't the bodies we had in high school or when we first married.

Although you know it's *you* standing in front of the mirror, you almost don't recognize yourself. And if you're going to a reunion you wonder whether anyone else will recognize you. It's a good thing they place senior yearbook pictures on nametags at high school reunions, or you wouldn't have a clue whom you were talking to!

Unfortunately, most people don't age gracefully. Hearing loss, fading eyesight, and creaking joints accompany our advancing years. Getting older reminds me of what Jesus said to Peter:

> I tell you the truth, when you were young, you were able to do as you liked; you dressed yourself and went wherever you wanted to go. But when you are old, you will stretch out your hands, and others will dress you and take you where you don't want to go. (John 21:18 NLT)

If and when we get to the stage described by Jesus we'll hardly recognize ourselves anymore, nor will those who knew us in the vibrancy of our youth.

When it comes to the next life, we are naturally curious

as to who we will be in heaven. Will we be ourselves? And if so, which self—the young, energetic go-getter or the old, lethargic individual with hardly enough get up to go? Will we recognize friends and family, and will they recognize us—and which version of "us" will they know?

These are intriguing questions. However, before we answer them it is important to understand some important truths about the resurrection of the dead.

Will Everyone Receive a Resurrection Body?

At funerals, I sometimes hear people say things like, "This isn't the real Mary. This is only her shell. The real Mary—her spirit—is in heaven." Or, "This is the last time we'll ever see Roger in this body." It's natural to say things like this because we know that our earthly bodies are temporal and our spirits are eternal.

However, those realities have led many Christians to the wrong conclusion that there is a dichotomy between our bodies (what some believe are only the appearance of who we are) and our spirits (what they believe are the reality of who we are). They believe that since we leave our earthly bodies behind at death, we will exist in heaven as disembodied spirits.

Nothing could be further from the truth. In the new heaven and new earth we will not exist as sanctified versions of Casper the Friendly Ghost. Instead, just as we possess physical bodies in this world, we will also exist and relate to one another in physical bodies in the next world. How do I know that? Consider how God designed us and what His plans are for us.

God's Design: Body and Spirit

Throughout this book we've seen that heaven is primarily the re-creation of the original Eden—the earth as God originally designed it. If that is true, then it seems reasonable to assume that the residents of the new earth will exist in the same form as the original occupants of Eden. When we turn to Genesis 2 we find a very interesting statement about God's creation of the first couple:

> Then the LORD God formed man of dust from the ground, and breathed into his nostrils the breath of life; and man became a living being. (Gen. 2:7)

When God created Adam—and later Eve—He fashioned them as physical beings (dust) into whom He placed His Spirit (the breath of life), making each person a "living being." Notice that a person needs both a body and a spirit to be considered a "living being." Without a physical body he or she would not be a "being," and without a spirit he or she would not be "living." God created Adam—and every person since—as body and spirit.

Of course, there is a time coming when every human being will have his or her spirit separated from his or her physical body. The word *death* comes from the Greek word *thanatos*, which means "to separate." Death is the separation of our spirit from our physical bodies. As we saw in chapter 4, at that moment of separation the spirit of a Christian goes immediately into the presence of Jesus Christ, while the spirit of a non-Christian goes immediately to hades, the temporary place of torment.

But how long will that separation of body and spirit last?

As we also saw in chapter 4, some theologians speculate that at death, both Christians and non-Christians will receive some kind of temporary bodies while awaiting their eternal bodies. After all, they argue, God originally created us as body and spirit, and in eternity we will be body and spirit. Why would we think that in the intermediate state we would be disembodied spirits?

Others believe, since there is no direct evidence in the Bible that Christians and non-Christians who die will receive bodies before the final resurrection, we should assume that during the time between our deaths and the receiving of our new bodies we will exist as spirits only.

God's Plan: Two Resurrections

But here is one thing we know for sure: in the future, every Christian and non-Christian will receive a new physical body that is designed to experience the eternal pleasures of heaven or torments of hell. The Scripture repeatedly talks about the resurrection of both the righteous and unrighteous. For example, the patriarch Job believed he would see God with his own physical eyes when he declared:

> Even after my skin is destroyed,
> Yet from my flesh I shall see God. (Job 19:26)

The prophet Daniel believed that both the wicked and the righteous would be resurrected to receive their just rewards:

> Many of those who sleep in the dust of the ground will awake, these [believers] to everlasting life, but the others [unbelievers] to disgrace and everlasting contempt. (Dan. 12:2)

When will these resurrections of our bodies take place?

The First Resurrection

The Bible uses the term *first resurrection* to describe the time when all believers will receive their brand-new bodies for eternity. The apostle John wrote, "Blessed and holy is the one who has a part in the first resurrection; over these the second death has no power" (Rev. 20:6).

It is important to understand that the first resurrection does not occur at a single point in time. Instead, different groups of Christians will receive their new bodies at different times in the future. Paul explained: "For as in Adam all die, so also in Christ all will be made alive. But *each in his own order*" (1 Cor. 15:22–23).

The Greek word translated "order" is *tagma*, and refers to a military procession, with each corps falling in at its appointed time. At death every Christian's spirit is immediately ushered into the presence of God, but we do not receive our new bodies until our assigned time or "order." The chart on page 151 illustrates the various times different groups of Christians will receive the new bodies they will inhabit for eternity.

The Second Resurrection

While believers will participate in the first resurrection, every unbeliever since Adam will be part of what we might call the *second resurrection*. Unlike the first resurrection, the second resurrection will occur at a single point in time—prior to the judgment of all unbelievers at an event commonly known as the great white throne judgment:

What Happens to a Person after Death[2]

	At Death	Bodily Resurrection	Judgment	Eternal Destination
Old Testament Believer	Paradise/ Abraham's Bosom — The Grave	Resurrection at Christ's Second Coming	Judgment on Earth for Rewards	Heaven
Christian	Christ's Presence — The Grave	Resurrection at the Rapture	Judgment Seat of Christ in Heaven for Rewards	Heaven
Millennial Believer	Christ's Presence — The Grave	Resurrection at the End of the Millennium	Judgment on Earth for Rewards	Heaven
Tribulation Believer	Christ's Presence — The Grave	Resurrection at Christ's Second Coming	Judgment on Earth for Rewards	Heaven
Unbeliever	Sheol/Hades Torment — The Grave	Resurrection at the End of the Millennium	Judgment at the Great White Throne for Sins	Hell/Gehenna/ Lake of Fire

And the sea gave up the dead which were in it, and death and Hades [the temporary residing place of all the unsaved dead] gave up the dead which were in them; and they were judged, every one of them according to their deeds. Then death and Hades were thrown into the lake of fire. This is the second death, the lake of fire. (Rev. 20:13–14)

Just as Christians will receive physical bodies in which they can enjoy the eternal benefits of the new heaven and new earth, unbelievers will be resurrected and receive physical bodies in which to endure the eternal torment of the lake of fire.

How Is a Physical Resurrection Possible?

First Corinthians 15 is the most complete explanation of the resurrection in the Bible. The apostle Paul answers many questions we naturally have about the resurrection and the nature of our new bodies. For example, anticipating objections to a physical resurrection, the apostle Paul writes: "Someone will say, 'How are the dead raised?'" (1 Cor. 15:35).

Perhaps you have wondered the same thing. I want to be sensitive here, but I'm often asked about those whose bodies have been destroyed in an accident or a tragedy, such as the victims of September 11, 2001. How can their disintegrated bodies be resurrected? Or consider the passengers in an airliner that explodes over the ocean. The bodies of dismembered passengers are submerged in the water only to be eaten by sea creatures.

When Roger Williams, the founder of Rhode Island, died, he was buried at the foot of an apple tree. When his body was disinterred years later, the roots of the tree had penetrated his casket, grown through the top of his skull, and branched out down his arms and legs. The tree had literally consumed Williams's body, deriving nourishment from his corpse. So how is Roger Williams's body ever going to be resurrected?

Or consider what happens to the person who at death donates a part of his or her body to a worthy recipient. How can that person ever reclaim his or her vital organs if an eye went to Ethel and a kidney was donated to Sydney? This puts Paul's question in 1 Corinthians 15:35 in a new light, doesn't it? How could a decomposed body—scattered at sea, eaten by fish, consumed by an apple tree, or dissected for its organs—ever be put back together and returned to the original owner? Theologian John Calvin answered the question this way: "Since God has all the elements at his disposal, no difficulty can prevent him from commanding the earth, the fire, and the water to give up what they seem to have destroyed."[3]

The Analogy: Planting and Harvesting

Paul answered his own question about the possibility of a resurrection by using an analogy familiar to his audience: the planting and harvesting of a crop.

> That which you sow does not come to life unless it dies; and that which you sow, you do not sow the body which is to be, but a bare grain, perhaps of wheat or of something else. But God gives it a body just as He wished, and to each of the seeds a body of its own. (vv. 36–38)

Before a watermelon seed ever produces a watermelon it must first be placed in the ground, where it dies. When a farmer goes into the field to gather the harvest, he or she doesn't gather watermelon seeds but something much better—watermelons! The harvest is always superior to what was planted.

So it is with the resurrection. When we die, our human bodies are like "seeds" that are planted in the ground. The death of our human bodies—regardless of how it occurs—is not a hindrance to a future resurrection but a prerequisite for a greater "harvest." Why?

Notice Paul's words: "That which you sow does not come to life unless it dies" (1 Cor. 15:36). The apostle goes on to explain that our old bodies must die because they are not designed for eternity. "Flesh and blood cannot inherit the kingdom of God," Paul said, "nor does the perishable inherit the imperishable" (v. 50). While your body is perfectly designed for planet Earth, it is not suited for Mars, Pluto, or heaven. That is why we should not view death as "the end" of something great but as "the beginning" of something greater.

The body we receive at "harvest time"—the resurrection— is vastly superior to the body that is planted in the ground. Think of it this way: imagine it's a scorching summer day— 100 degrees in the shade. You've been outside working in the yard. To cool down, you come into the house and open the refrigerator for something refreshing. Which would you rather sink your teeth into—a slice of ice-cold watermelon or an ice-cold watermelon seed?

Similarly, when our bodies are resurrected from the grave, it will not be our old bodies that are raised. The resurrection is not a reconstruction but a re-creation of our bodies. Those who have been blown apart, or cremated, or donated their organs to others won't be rebuilt versions of their dead selves any more than a watermelon is a rebuilt version of a watermelon seed. Rather, they are something new and vastly superior—the watermelon itself.

Superior but Similar

Although the "harvest" is *superior* to the "seed," the harvest is also *similar* to the seed. You don't plant a watermelon seed and harvest a kumquat! A watermelon seed produces a watermelon. Similarly, your new body that is raised at "harvest" time will not be something completely unlike your body that was buried at death. You don't die and become someone else in the resurrection. There will be some similarities between our earthly bodies and our heavenly bodies.

The perfect example of this is Jesus's resurrection body. And since Scripture promises that the bodies of resurrected believers will be like His (1 John 3:2), we should look closely at Jesus's resurrection body if we want to discover what our bodies will be like in the new heaven and the new earth.

Was Jesus's Resurrection Spiritual or Physical?

Of course, what follows in this section assumes that Christ's body was actually raised from the dead. Some members of the Corinthian church questioned whether anyone could physically come back from the dead. They had no problem believing that the spirit of Christ lived on—His moral example, His wise teaching, and His loving attitude—but were unsure that *He* lived again body and soul. But Paul consistently proclaimed the physical death and resurrection of Christ as the foundation stone of the gospel:

> I delivered to you as of first importance what I also received, that Christ died for our sins according to the Scriptures, and that He was buried, and that He was raised on the third day according to the Scriptures. (1 Cor. 15:3–4)

Paul went on to argue that if this was *untrue*—if Christ hadn't died and wasn't raised from the dead—then the consequences were too terrible to contemplate.[4] Preaching would be worthless—hollow words of no consequence. Faith would be futile—we might as well believe in fairies and pixie dust. Christians would be charlatans—no better than cultists or used-car salespersons who lie. Sin would be unforgiven—you're on your own before the judgment of God. Death would result in damnation, not salvation. Christians would be pathetic—fools and knaves to have believed such nonsense. Practically speaking, if Christ's body still lies in a Jerusalem tomb we might as well give up on Christ and sleep in on Sunday mornings.

"But now Christ has been raised from the dead," Paul declared (v. 20). And what proof did Paul offer? Christ in His resurrection body "appeared to Cephas [Peter], then to the twelve. After that He appeared to more than five hundred brethren at one time . . . then He appeared to James, then to all the apostles; and last of all . . . He appeared to me also" (vv. 5–8). In fact, Scripture lists seventeen different appearances of the resurrected Jesus in bodily form.

On the day of His resurrection, Jesus appeared five times:

1. To Mary Magdalene (Mark 16:9–11; John 20:11–17)
2. To the other women (Matt. 28:8–10)
3. To Peter (Luke 24:34; 1 Cor. 15:5)

4. To the disciples on the road to Emmaus
   (Mark 16:12–13; Luke 24:13–35)
5. To the ten disciples, without Thomas
   (Mark 16:14; Luke 24:36–43; John 20:19–23)[5]

Over the next thirty-nine days, Jesus presented Himself to His disciples six times:

1. To the eleven disciples a week later, with Thomas (John 20:26–29)
2. To seven disciples by the Sea of Galilee (John 21:1–14)
3. To more than five hundred believers (1 Cor. 15:6)
4. To James, Jesus's brother (1 Cor. 15:7)
5. To the eleven disciples in Galilee (Matt. 28:16–20)
6. To the eleven disciples at the ascension in Jerusalem (Mark 16:19–20; Luke 24:50–53; Acts 1:3–9)

And before the final book of the Bible was written, Jesus appeared an additional six times:

1. To Stephen at his martyrdom (Acts 7:55–56)
2. To Saul at his conversion on the road to Damascus (Acts 9:3–7)
3. To Paul in Arabia (Gal. 1:12)
4. To Paul in the Jerusalem temple (Acts 22:17–21)
5. To Paul in prison at Caesarea (Acts 23:11)
6. To the apostle John on the island of Patmos (Rev. 1:12–20)

But Jesus did more than just show up and say, "*Shalom,* y'all." He conversed with His disciples on all seventeen occasions. He ate with His disciples on at least three occasions: after the encounter on the Emmaus road, during the visit with the ten (without Thomas), and at breakfast by the seashore. And on two occasions His disciples touched His body: the women who came to the tomb to anoint Him, and Mary Magdalene. Other times Jesus invited people to touch Him, including the disciples on the Emmaus road and Thomas. Jesus's physical appearance—especially His scars—was enough to convince Thomas that Jesus had been resurrected and was truly the Son of God. "Thomas answered and said to [Jesus], 'My Lord and my God!'" (John 20:28).

The disciples didn't interact with just Jesus's disembodied spirit after the resurrection but with Jesus Himself in bodily form.

What Was Jesus's Resurrection Body Like?

When Jesus received His new (postresurrection) body, it was both different from and similar to His old (preresurrection) body. Jesus's new body was superior to His earthly body as demonstrated by His ability to materialize at will—even through locked doors. This happened at least twice during the forty days Jesus walked around in His new body. The first time occurred on resurrection day. The disciples were shut up behind closed doors, fearing the Jews might find and crucify them, when, unexpectedly, "Jesus came and stood in their midst and said to them, 'Peace be with you'" (v. 19). The second time occurred a week later, when Jesus appeared to Thomas, who was "inside . . . the doors having been shut" (v. 26).

Because Jesus could appear at will, He could also disappear at will. The best example of this comes from the dinner in Emmaus after His resurrection. After explaining from the Old Testament Scriptures why the Messiah must suffer and die, Jesus sat down to share a meal with two disciples. "When He had reclined at the table with them," Luke wrote, "He took the bread and blessed it, and breaking it, He began giving it to them. Then their eyes were opened and they recognized Him; and He vanished from their sight" (Luke 24:30–31).

But there were also similarities between His new and old body—enough so that when He appeared to His followers in His new body they eventually recognized Him. I say "eventually" because there were instances in which the disciples did not immediately recognize the Lord—for understandable reasons. Some were so full of sorrow they couldn't see clearly (John 20:11–15). One appearance happened while it was still dark (20:1, 14–15). On another occasion the distance between Jesus and His disciples was great enough to obscure recognizable features (21:4). Some were disbelieving (20:24–25), while those behind closed doors were startled when He suddenly appeared (Luke 24:36–37). Finally, others were spiritually dull (vv. 25–26). Yet in all these cases the confusion was merely temporary.

Eventually, the similarities between Jesus's natural body and His new body caused His followers to recognize Him. Maybe the similarity was something as trivial as the way He tore apart a piece of bread. After speaking with the disciples on the Emmaus road, Jesus ate dinner with them—just like a man. But Luke records that "He was recognized by them in the breaking of the bread" (v. 35). Perhaps Jesus held the bread in His right hand as He tore it with His other hand because the Lord was left-handed in His natural body. If Jesus were left-handed in His natural body there would be no reason for Him to be right-handed in His resurrection body. His physical features, postresurrection, were similar to His preresurrection features—the nail holes in His hands and feet prove that.

What Will Our Resurrection Bodies Be Like?

Why this detailed examination of Jesus's resurrection body? Scripture promises that our resurrection bodies will be like Jesus's:

> Beloved, now we are children of God, and it has not appeared as yet what we will be. We know that when He appears, *we will be like Him*, because we will see Him just as He is. (1 John 3:2)

In Colossians 1:18 Paul referred to Jesus's resurrection as "the firstborn from the dead." The word translated "firstborn" comes from the Greek word from which we get our English word *prototype*. Whenever a manufacturer builds a new automobile or airplane, they first build a prototype. Every other car and plane is then patterned after that first one. In the same way, Jesus's resurrection body was an example of what our bodies are going to be like.

So in what specific ways will our new resurrection bodies be in "conformity with the body of His glory," as Paul promised in Philippians 3:21?

Our Bodies Will Be Physical

After making the case for the resurrection of Christ and the resurrection of believers in 1 Corinthians 15:1–19, Paul addressed the question of what kind of resurrection bodies we'll receive in verses 39–50. The simple answer is that we'll have different bodies than the ones we now inhabit—as different as the bodies of animals, stars, and plants are from each other. Paul explained:

> All flesh is not the same flesh, but there is one flesh of men, and another flesh of beasts, and another flesh of birds, and another of fish. There are also heavenly bodies and earthly bodies, but the glory of the heavenly is one, and the glory of the earthly is another. There is one glory of the sun, and another glory of the moon, and another glory of the stars; for star differs from star in glory. (1 Cor. 15:39–41)

Paul's point is this: the body of a fish is not the body of a bird; the body of a bird is not the body of a beast; the body of a beast is not the body of a human (a truth that obviously is contrary to the basic premise of evolution). A star is not a planet and a moon is not a star. Each one follows its own kind, just as God intended at the beginning of the creation.

Similarly, our heavenly bodies will differ from our earthly bodies. Why should we find it difficult to believe that there is one kind of body created for inhabiting earth and another kind of body for inhabiting heaven? But to ensure that we wouldn't misunderstand, Paul detailed the difference between our earthly and heavenly bodies:

> So also is the resurrection of the dead. It is sown a perishable body, it is raised an imperishable body; it is sown in dishonor, it is raised in glory; it is sown in weakness, it is raised in power; it is sown a natural body, it is raised a spiritual body. If there is a natural body, there is also a spiritual body. (vv. 42–44)

The Greek word for "body" used here is *soma*. In every instance in the New Testament, *soma* refers to a physical body. So, when Paul used *soma* in verse 44, in reference to the "natural body" and "spiritual body," he made clear that our resurrection bodies would be just as physical as our natural bodies are physical.

But just because our heavenly bodies will be physical doesn't mean they will be physical in the same way our earthly bodies are. For example:

- Our earthly bodies decay; our heavenly bodies will endure.
- Our earthly bodies are infected with sin; our heavenly bodies will be free of sin.
- Our earthly bodies are weak; our heavenly bodies will be powerful.
- Our earthly bodies are for the old earth; our heavenly bodies are for the new earth.

The differences between our earthly bodies and our heavenly bodies often lead people to ask whether we will eat and drink or wear clothes in heaven. And what age will we be? As with all questions about our resurrection bodies, we must look to the resurrection body of Jesus for answers since He is the pattern—the *protokos*—of our resurrection bodies.

We've already seen, on at least three specific occasions, that the resurrected Jesus shared a meal with His disciples. But even before Jesus's death and resurrection He promised His disciples they would gather at His banquet table and feast with Him during the millennial kingdom. "Just as My

Father has granted Me a kingdom, I grant you that you may eat and drink at My table in My kingdom" (Luke 22:29–30). Obviously this event during the millennium occurs after Jesus's and the disciples' resurrections, when they are living in their new bodies. This promise indicates that we, too, will share meals with Jesus and the disciples in our new bodies.

We'll also wear clothes in heaven. Some object to this idea because Adam and Eve, before the fall, didn't wear clothes. Although life on the new earth will be Eden-like, it won't be like the popular survival show *Naked and Afraid*, in which a man and woman attempt to survive in the wild for twenty-one days without clothes.

When John saw the resurrected Christ on Patmos, Jesus was "clothed in a robe reaching to the feet, and girded across His chest with a golden sash" (Rev. 1:13). And when Christ spoke to the church at Sardis, He told them: "He who overcomes will thus be clothed in white garments" (3:5), which John confirmed with his own eyes (7:9).

When the bride of Christ—the church—is presented to Jesus at His second coming, we will be clothed in "fine linen, bright and clean" (19:8). And when Jesus, the conquering King, comes to finalize His war with evil, it is said He will be "clothed with a robe dipped in blood" (v. 13).

We will also retain our sexual identity in our new bodies. Some have wrongly concluded that we'll be androgynous in heaven—genderless—because Paul claimed, "there is neither . . . male nor female . . . in Christ Jesus" (Gal. 3:28). But Paul wasn't referring to the sexual nature of our bodies in the next life. He was referring to our equality in Christ—in this life. The fact that some people did not recognize the resurrected Lord immediately (like the two on the road to

Emmaus) strongly argues that Jesus looked like any other man instead of some "otherworldly" sexless alien.

Our bodies will probably be resurrected at an ideal, youthful, and mature age. Though we can't be sure, many theologians believe we'll be in our thirties. Thirty is considered the peak of perfection, both mentally and physically. (I think I remember that!) It was the age when Old Testament priests began their ministry in the temple and when Christ began His public ministry. So, for those of us a little bit older, go back and look at old pictures and imagine your eternal self when you were thirty. And for those younger than thirty, including children . . . well, you have something to look forward to!

Our Bodies Will Be Perfect

We will have real, physical bodies. But, as we've seen, they will be different than the bodies we inhabit today—they will be free from sin and therefore free from disease, decay, and death. Remember, in heaven, "the first things [the things of the earth] have passed away" (Rev. 21:4). Cancer, heart attacks, and strokes will all be a thing of the past. So will blindness, deafness, and paralysis, as well as gray hair, wrinkles, and widening girths. Missing limbs will be restored. From the top of our heads to the bottom of our feet, we'll be perfect in every way.

"Can you imagine the hope this gives someone spinal cord–injured like me?" my friend Joni Eareckson Tada asked. "Or someone who is cerebral palsied, brain-injured, or who has multiple sclerosis? Imagine the hope this gives someone who is manic depressive. No other religion, no other philosophy promises new bodies, hearts, and minds. Only in the Gospel of Christ do hurting people find such incredible hope."[6]

We can assume that our resurrection bodies will be attractive and retain the same physical traits of our individual bodies today.[7] In other words, not every man will have the physique of a bodybuilder and the looks of a movie star. Nor will women have the shape of a fashion model and the face of an angel. Your face will be your face. Your body will be your body—tall, short, thin, or plump. But all will be healthy and appealing. We won't have to worry about body image, comparing ourselves with others. Plastic surgeons will not be needed in heaven. Nor will cosmetics—sorry all you Mary Kay–ers. As one writer claims, "We won't have to *try* to look beautiful—we *will* be beautiful."[8]

Our Bodies Will Be Personal

Your body, your memories, your gifts and talents, your passions, and your spirit are what make you *you*. In the resurrection, all of these will be perfected and glorified, "in the twinkling of an eye" (1 Cor. 15:52). But you won't become someone else or something else (like an angel). You will become the *you* God intended you to be.

When John wrote that we "will be like [Jesus]" (1 John 3:2), the apostle didn't mean that we will become mini-Christs, like Dr. Evil's "Mini-Me" in the Austin Powers movies. We will become like Christ in character and with a similar heavenly DNA, but we'll retain our distinctive personalities. In heaven, I'll be Robert Jeffress—only perfected. And if you're a believer, you'll be Sandy Smith or Bob Brown or [insert your name]—only perfected.

Think of it like this: you probably have a computer and use certain software for word processing or developing spreadsheets. When an upgrade becomes available, you don't get a whole new program; you get a better version of the same program—only with new and better features. Likewise, with our resurrection we'll have upgrades, including new features (though without the glitches or programming errors), but we'll still be who we are.

This was Jesus's point when He appeared to the disciples after the resurrection and said, "It is I Myself" (Luke 24:39). Who He was before His death and resurrection is who He is after His death and resurrection. Randy Alcorn made a strong case for continuity when he wrote:

> If we weren't ourselves in the afterlife then we couldn't be held accountable for what we did in this life. The Judgment would be meaningless. If Barbara is no longer Barbara, she can't be rewarded or held accountable for anything Barbara did. She'd have to say, "But that wasn't me." The doctrines of judgment and eternal rewards depend on people's retaining their distinct identities from this life to the next.[9]

Part of our distinctive identity is that we'll keep our own individual names in heaven. God promised the righteous citizens of Israel that their individual names would endure throughout eternity:

> "For just as the new heavens and the new earth
> Which I make will endure before Me," declares the
> LORD,
> "So your offspring and your name will endure."
> (Isa. 66:22)

And Jesus called those currently in heaven by their earthly names. "I say to you that many will come from east and west, and recline at the table with Abraham, Isaac and Jacob in the kingdom of heaven" (Matt. 8:11).

But some will also be given additional names in heaven. Speaking to the church at Pergamum, the resurrected Christ said, "To him who overcomes . . . I will give him a white stone, and a new name written on the stone which no one knows but he who receives it" (Rev. 2:17). These new names don't invalidate our old names, nor do they erase our personality. In fact, these new names reflect the true personality and responsibility of those who receive them. For example, Jacob, which means "heel-catcher" or "supplanter," was also Israel—"one who strives with God." Simon, which means "God has heard," was also Peter—"the rock." And Saul, which means "prayed for," was also Paul—"small" or "humble."

We've looked at a lot of details concerning our resurrection bodies. But what does it all mean? Simply this: when we get to heaven we'll recognize each other as the unique individuals we are. We'll even recognize saints whom we've never seen before. Peter, James, and John recognized Moses and Elijah when they appeared with Jesus at His transfiguration (Matt. 17:4).

The relationships we have formed on earth will continue in heaven. But they will continue without strife or enmity. In heaven, all things are made new. "Our eternal reunion with Christian loved ones and friends will be ceaselessly glorious," theologian Ron Rhodes wrote.

Keep in mind that we will no longer have sin natures. There will be no fights among loved ones. There won't be any resentment or envy or jealousy. There won't be any one-upmanship or rivalries. There won't be any cross words or misunderstanding or selfishness. Our relationships in heaven will truly be wonderful and utterly satisfying.[10]

Now that is something truly to look forward to in that "place called heaven."

8

Will Heaven Be the Same for Everyone?

Behold, I am coming quickly, and My reward is with Me, to render to every man according to what he has done.

Revelation 22:12

Jim Marshall was a defensive lineman on the Minnesota Vikings' famed "Purple People Eaters" in the 1960s and '70s. Though a Super Bowl champion, Marshall is best known for the mistake he made on October 24, 1964. In a game against the San Francisco 49ers Marshall saw a fumble, picked up the football, and began running the length of the field. Vikings players on the sidelines followed Marshall and began yelling . . . for him to run the other way! Marshall didn't realize he was running toward his own end zone. In spite of that mistake, Marshall played so well that the Vikings ended up winning the game 27–22.

But history has a way of recording the worst. Few people

remember Marshall's outstanding performance in the game, only his major mistake. In fact, to this day Jim Marshall is remembered by the nickname he earned that day: "Wrong Way" Marshall.

Making it to the end zone is the goal of football. But making it to the *right* end zone is the key to winning. A similar truth applies to heaven. Making it to heaven is the goal, but making it there to hear Jesus say, "Well done, good and faithful servant" is the key to ultimate victory.

While all true Christians will cross the spiritual end zone, many will enter only after spending some time running the wrong way. Some believers will be celebrated for how they played the game of life. But others who were ultimately on the winning side will still be evaluated as having done little to contribute to the success of the team.

It's a hard but inescapable truth: heaven will not be the same for every Christian. When "we . . . all stand before the judgment seat of God" (Rom. 14:10), some will receive great rewards and others will not.

A Divine Summons

Every person from the time of Adam to the present will have to appear before the divine Judge who "[will] judge the living and the dead" (2 Tim. 4:1). No one escapes God's judgment. As the writer of Hebrews declared, "it is appointed for men to die once and after this comes judgment" (Heb. 9:27). Notice the writer doesn't limit the generic term "men" (meaning "human beings") to only certain individuals or groups. Everyone will face God's scrutiny of his or her life.

However, there is not one single judgment for all humankind.

Instead, unbelievers will stand before Christ at what is called the great white throne judgment. This judgment is for all unbelievers since the time of Adam and will occur at the end of the millennial kingdom, resulting in condemnation—being cast into the lake of fire (Rev. 20:11–15). Believers will appear before a very different judgment, "the judgment seat of Christ" (2 Cor. 5:10), resulting in commendation for those the Lord deems to have served Him faithfully in their brief existence on earth.

An Appearance before the Judge

A few years ago, members from our church toured the ancient city of Corinth, where Paul spent eighteen months preaching the gospel. Many Corinthians came to faith in Christ through the apostle's preaching. However, others were incensed by Paul's message and dragged him before the Roman governor of the province:

> But while Gallio was proconsul of Achaia, the Jews with one accord rose up against Paul and brought him before the judgment seat, saying, "This man persuades men to worship God contrary to the law." But when Paul was about to open his mouth, Gallio said to the Jews, "If it were a matter of wrong or of vicious crime, O Jews, it would be reasonable for me to put up with you; but if there are questions about words and names and your own law, look after it yourselves; I am unwilling to be a judge of these matters." And he drove them away from the judgment seat. (Acts 18:12–16)

The phrase translated "judgment seat" is the Greek word *bema*. It refers to a raised platform on which a ruler or judge sat to pronounce decrees or verdicts, similar to the raised bench judges sit at in modern courthouses.

As our group stood on the spot where Paul faced his judge, I wondered what it must have been like to be in Paul's sandals—standing before a man who held his fate in his hands. How did the apostle maintain his cool demeanor when facing his possible death? I think it's because Paul understood that Gallio's judgment—whatever it was—wasn't the final judgment on his life. One day Paul would stand before another judgment seat from which the Judge of the universe would evaluate Paul's faithfulness to Christ.

What makes the *bema* seat judgment different than the great white throne judgment is that everyone who stands before the judgment seat of Christ will be saved. No one will appear at this judgment who hasn't already been declared "not guilty" by God. The theological term for this declaration is *justification*. "Therefore, having been justified by faith," Paul wrote, "we have peace with God through our Lord Jesus Christ" (Rom. 5:1).

Think of justification this way: imagine you use your debit card to make a purchase, but in so doing you overdraw your account. The bank notifies you of the overdraft and applies a penalty for covering the purchase. If you will deposit the amount of the overdraft and penalty, the bank will forgive the debt and won't levy an additional penalty. The only problem is that you are bankrupt and have no funds to deposit. You are in a deficit position with the bank. However, a friend finds out about your dilemma and makes a deposit to your account to cover the overdraft and penalty.

In a sense, that is what Christ offers to do for us. All of us are "overdrawn" in our "righteousness" account before

God. And every time we sin we only increase our indebtedness to God. If we die spiritually bankrupt—unable to pay our debt—we face the penalty of eternal separation from God.

But when we trust in Christ for our salvation God credits our "righteousness" account with the perfection of His Son, erasing our debt and eliminating any future penalty. That means Christians never have to worry about a future judgment for the sins already paid for by Christ. Paul assures us that "there is now no condemnation for those who are in Christ Jesus" (Rom. 8:1).

However, justification does not exempt us from God's evaluation of our lives after we are forgiven for our sins. Paul declares:

> We must *all* appear before the judgment seat of Christ, so that each one may be recompensed for his deeds in the body, according to what he has done, whether good or bad. (2 Cor. 5:10)

Notice Paul said, "We must *all* appear." I've checked the Greek text and "all" means "all!" Every believer will appear before Christ's bench—there are no exceptions, exclusions, or exemptions. Each of us will appear before the Lord for an evaluation to receive whatever reward is appropriate. *Remember, the judgment seat of Christ is for the* commendation *of believers while the great white throne judgment is for the* condemnation *of unbelievers.* This is why Paul told the Corinthians to make it their "ambition, whether at home [in the body] or absent [from the body], to be pleasing to Him" (2 Cor. 5:9).

When Will Our Judgment Take Place?

When will this evaluation take place? Most probably it will occur right after the rapture of the church, when living Christians are immediately transported into the presence of the Lord and dead believers are resurrected to eternal life. While no single verse indicates that the *bema* seat judgment occurs immediately after the rapture, a number of factors point to this conclusion.

First, the twenty-four elders mentioned in Revelation 4:10 (who represent all believers) are portrayed in heaven as having already received their rewards (crowns) at the beginning of the tribulation. Additionally, when the church (the "bride of Christ") returns to earth with Jesus at the second coming—seven years after the rapture—the bride is said to be clothed in "fine linen, bright and clean," which represents "the righteous acts of the saints" (Rev. 19:8). Both of these facts imply that the evaluation of Christians' lives has already occurred.

Do Our Works Really Matter?

Many Christians are confused about the importance of obedience to God in this life. "My good works are worthless to God," they mistakenly claim. While it's true we are saved by God's grace apart from our works, God rewards us as Christians based on our works. While our works are worthless in securing us a *place* in heaven, they are integral in determining our *experience* in heaven.

Paul drew a distinction between works *before* salvation and works *after* salvation. This is what he said about our works before salvation: "For by grace you have been saved through faith; and that not of yourselves, it is the gift of God; *not as a result of works*, so that no one may boast" (Eph. 2:8–9).

And this is what Paul said about works after salvation: "For we are His workmanship, created in Christ Jesus *for good works*, which God prepared beforehand so that we would walk in them" (v. 10).

Before we became a Christian, our works were only sufficient to condemn us before God. But once we have become a Christian, our works should be sufficient to commend us to God. As we've already seen, we will all appear before the judgment seat of Christ and be evaluated on our works, "whether good or bad" (2 Cor. 5:10). The Greek word translated "bad" (*phaulos*) literally means "worthless."

If you think Google, Facebook, and Amazon collect a mountain of information on search histories, likes, and purchases, their data collection is a molehill compared to God's collection system. He knows every word spoken, every thought contemplated, every action taken, and every motive held. And one day He will bring it all to light. According to Scripture, the Lord will evaluate our actions, thoughts, and words; our use of talents, gifts, and time; as well as our treatment of others, hospitality to strangers, responses to mistreatment, efforts to win others to Christ, and attitude toward money.[1]

Nothing will be hidden from the Lord's scrutiny. Thinking about that future day of God's evaluation reminds me of a very thorough physical exam I once had (the operative word being "once"). Part of the examination entailed determining my body fat. The doctor's assistant instructed me to remove my clothes and get into a basket to be submerged into what is appropriately called "the fat tank." As I held my breath underwater, the doctor calculated my percentage of body fat.

But that wasn't the worst part. I was then forced to stand completely naked in front of my doctor while he used some sort of torture device to pinch different parts of my body to calculate body fat utilizing a different method. In that moment, I regretted every chocolate chip cookie I had ever eaten, every morning I had rolled over and hit my snooze alarm instead of hitting the treadmill, and every midnight trip to the freezer for another scoop of ice cream. Standing there without a stitch of clothing on, being pinched, poked, and prodded, while my doctor frowned, scowled, and grinned, caused me to think one thought: *He knows everything!*

At the end of this ordeal my doctor called me into his office. After a few pleasantries, he opened the file containing the results of my examination. First, he complimented me on my exercise program, the results of the stress test, and the bowl of Bran Flakes I ate every morning for breakfast. Then the corners of his mouth turned downward, and he got serious. "Now, let's talk about your body fat." *That's always a pleasant subject for conversation*, I thought. "You need to melt a few points off of that. And your cholesterol needs to be lowered, so quit eating that bowl of ice cream every night." While my doctor commended me for the good things I was doing, he also offered a critique of the not-so-good habits that were endangering my health. My exam wasn't the most enjoyable experience of my life but it wasn't the worst experience either.

Similarly, when we stand before the Lord's judgment seat every aspect of our lives will be laid bare before God. As Jesus warned, "For nothing is hidden that will not become evident, nor anything secret that will not be known and come to light" (Luke 8:17). God's frank evaluation of the totality of our brief time on earth will result in rewards or the forfeiture of rewards—but not in eternal condemnation.

What Actually Happens at the Judgment Seat of Christ?

Paul utilized three analogies to explain what will happen at the judgment seat of Christ. Paul's first illustration is that of a trust agreement with God:

> But you, why do you judge your brother? Or you again, why do you regard your brother with contempt? . . . So then each one of us shall give an account of himself to God. (Rom. 14:10, 12)

The idea of "giving an account" is built on the analogy of a trustee—one who is responsible and legally bound to administer something that belongs to another. At some future time, the trustee must give an account of how he or she managed that trust. For example, financial advisors serve as trustees of their clients' money. The money that these advisors invest doesn't belong to them—they are simply managers who oversee and hopefully multiply the owners' funds.

Similarly, all that we have is a trust from God: our lives, talents, skills, gifts, and opportunities. We don't own anything—we are simply managers who are responsible to use those assets to further God's interests. At the *bema* judgment we need to be prepared to answer the Lord's question, "What have you done with what I have entrusted to you?"

The trustee analogy highlights a basic but essential truth about how God will evaluate us at the judgment seat of Christ: God will not judge every Christian in the same way. For example, God will not judge me by the same standard by which He evaluates Billy Graham. God gave Dr. Graham a different gift than He has given to me. I don't have to worry that one day God will hold me accountable for opportunities that were never mine. A trustee is only responsible for that which has been entrusted to him or her.

Paul also utilizes the analogy of constructing a house as an illustration of the judgment Christians will face.

> According to the grace of God which was given to me, like a wise master builder I laid a foundation, and another is building on it. But each man must be careful how he builds on it. For no man can lay a foundation other than the one which is laid, which is Jesus Christ. (1 Cor. 3:10–11)

Every one of us is in the process of building our own "house" or life. The foundation of a Christian's life is his or her faith in Christ Jesus. However, once that foundation is laid we must determine what kind of life we construct, based on the building materials we choose. On the foundation of faith, believers can either build a life of "gold, silver, [and] precious stones" or we can choose "wood, hay, [and] straw" (v. 12).

When we stand before Christ, our lives—our houses—will be tested by fire: "each man's work will become evident; for the day will show it because it is to be revealed with fire, and the fire itself will test the quality of each man's work" (v. 13). The idea here is that the primary basis of God's evaluation of our lives will be how eternally significant our lives prove to be.

The only way to withstand the searing heat of Jesus's judgment is to construct our lives with durable materials. Building a life in pursuit of profits, power, or pleasures is like building a house made of straw. But unlike the children's story of the three little pigs, Jesus doesn't huff and puff to blow the house down—He simply sets a match to it! Every aspect of our lives judged to be temporal rather than eternal will be consumed in the inferno of His holiness, leaving behind only a pile of ashes.

However, building a life dedicated to glorifying God (gold), introducing others to the Savior (silver), and demonstrating a love for God and others (precious stones) is like constructing a building of steel and marble—it will be unscorched by the heat of Jesus's evaluation.[2] What endures will be rewarded. "If any man's work which he has built on it remains, he will receive a reward," Paul told the Corinthians (1 Cor. 3:14). A person's actions that end up being consumed will be lost forever—though the individual will be saved: "If any man's work is burned up, he will suffer loss; but he himself will be saved, yet so as through fire" (v. 15).

This analogy emphasizes that our lives will be judged based on durability—the choices we make in constructing our lives. But the *whats* of life aren't the only criteria by which Christ will evaluate our lives. He will also judge the *whys* of our choices.

> Therefore do not go on passing judgment before the time, but wait until the Lord comes who will both bring to light the things hidden in the darkness and disclose *the motives of*

men's hearts; and then each man's praise will come to him from God. (1 Cor. 4:5)

For example, if I give money to God out of obedience, He counts it as gold. But if I give hoping that others will notice how generous I am, He counts it as straw. Motives matter—whether I'm sharing the gospel with someone, going on a mission trip, or demonstrating hospitality to a stranger. "All the ways of a man are clean in his own sight," Solomon wrote. "But the LORD weighs the motives" (Prov. 16:2).

Some might wonder if investing your life wisely in order to earn future rewards is a wrong motive itself. Not at all! Consider the example of Abraham. Why was he willing to obey God by uprooting his family and leaving his friends for some unknown and unfamiliar destination? The writer of Hebrews says Abraham "was looking for the city which has foundations, whose architect and builder is God" (Heb. 11:10). The only city God has ever or will ever design and build is the New Jerusalem that is yet to be revealed. In other words, Abraham's obedience to God in this life was in anticipation of a reward from God in the next life.

Or think about Moses's experience. The future leader of God's people voluntarily surrendered the perks of living in Pharaoh's household and instead chose "to endure ill-treatment with the people of God than to enjoy the passing pleasures of sin" (v. 25). Why did Moses make that heroic choice? Simply out of dedication to God?

No, the writer of Hebrews reveals that Moses's decision was based on an objective calculation. Moses was "considering the reproach of Christ greater riches than the treasures of Egypt; for he was looking to the reward" (v. 26). The word translated "considering" means "calculating." In other words, Moses did the math and determined that the short-term pleasures of this life were negligible compared to the eternal rewards of the next life that result from obeying God.

Make no mistake about it, both Moses's and Abraham's motivation for obedience was a future reward. And that is the essence of faith—believing that in the future God will reward us if we build our lives around serving Him and His Kingdom. As the writer of Hebrews declares:

> And without faith it is impossible to please Him, for he who comes to God must believe that He is and that He is a *rewarder* of those who seek Him. (Heb. 11:6)

Some may question their motives, but these two men understood what my friend Erwin Lutzer has said: "Rewards are always dependent on faithfulness."[3] In other words, Abraham's and Moses's faithfulness in looking for the city of God and the heavenly reward revealed that their motives were holy, because ultimately their motives were to see Christ.

Paul's third analogy of the judgment is that of a track meet. Addressing the Corinthians once again, Paul wrote:

> Do you not know that those who run in a race all run, but only one receives the prize? Run in such a way that you may win. Everyone who competes in the games exercises self-control in all things. They then do it to receive a perishable wreath, but we an imperishable. Therefore I run in such a way, as not without aim; I box in such a way, as not beating the air; but I discipline my body and make it my slave, so that, after I have preached to others, I myself will not be disqualified. (1 Cor. 9:24–27)

The Isthmian Games were held every two years in Corinth and included footraces and boxing matches. The winner of these contests was awarded a crown. But unlike the gold medals handed out to Olympic champions today, the winner's wreath at the Isthmia was made of parsley, wild celery, or pine boughs. It eventually wilted and dried. Paul's point was to encourage the Corinthians (and us) to run the race of life in such a way as to win an "imperishable" crown—a heavenly reward that will never decay or die.

Track meets have simple rules. First, the race begins when the official fires the starting gun. We begin our race of faith the moment we place our eternal trust in Christ, not before. Second, runners must stay on the track or be disqualified. Christians have a unique "course" God has designed for us, and that course has no shortcuts. Finally, runners must avoid distractions and keep their eyes on the finishing tape.

Australian runner John Landy was in a heated contest with Roger Bannister as to who could be the first to break the four-minute-mile barrier. Bannister did it on May 6, 1954. A few months later, Landy and Bannister met at the British and Empire Commonwealth Games. Landy set a blistering pace and was winning the race. However, as he came around the last turn, Landy looked over his left shoulder to find Bannister. But just as Landy peered over his left shoulder, Bannister passed him on his right-hand side, winning the race and beating his record-breaking time for the mile.

It's all too easy for any of us to become distracted from life's finishing line. Giving too much attention to that which has little eternal value—television, the news, Facebook, Twitter, video games—can cause us to lose sight of "the race that is set before us" (Heb. 12:1). None of these activities is wrong in and of itself, but these diversions can cause us to forfeit the prize God awards to those who finish the race well.

What Future Rewards Will Mean to Us

Many Christians will be happy just to make it to heaven—that'll be enough reward for them . . . or so they think. But our rewards—or lack of them—will profoundly impact what kind of heaven we will experience. "Everyone in heaven will be *fully* blessed," theologian Norm Geisler said, "but not everyone will be *equally* blessed. Every believer's cup will be full and running over, but not everyone's cup will be the same size."[4]

This is not only biblical; it is just. If Christ rewarded us all equally in heaven, regardless of our behavior on earth, He would be an unjust Judge. But He's not. Think of it like this: a mother of two teenage boys is in the kitchen baking cakes. She tells them that if they will clean up their rooms she will bake each of them their favorite cake. Later, when she goes upstairs, she sees that one son has hung up his clothes, picked up his underwear and placed them in his dresser, and vacuumed the carpet.

However, the other son is sitting among a pile of dirty T-shirts, smelly socks, and pizza boxes playing video games. Both enjoy having their own room and both will enjoy a wonderful home-cooked meal, but only one will enjoy his favorite dessert.

The same is true for us. Although our works play no part in obtaining salvation, they play an integral role in obtaining rewards in heaven. Jesus said, "My reward is with Me, to render to every man *according to what he has done*" (Rev. 22:12).

Similarly, Paul echoed the importance of works when he explained that at the judgment seat of Christ, every Christian will be rewarded "for his deeds in the body, *according to what he has done*" (2 Cor. 5:10).

What the Winners Win

Imagine you spent years training to run in the Boston Marathon and, after pouring every ounce of life you had into the race, you crossed the finish line first. How would you feel if the race officials said, "This year we decided to change the rules. Instead of awarding those who finished in first, second, and third place, we are going to simply give everyone a participation trophy. We thought that would be more fair." Fair? It is unfair not to recognize and reward those who make the necessary sacrifices to win a contest.

The same truth applies to rewards in heaven. Those who run the race well, who administer their trust faithfully, and who build their lives with gold, silver, and precious stones—all with the right motives—will receive what the Bible calls "crowns." Scripture speaks of at least five different crowns we might receive at the judgment seat of Christ.

First, the "imperishable" crown (1 Cor. 9:25) is for those who live a disciplined, Spirit-controlled life. Like the fruit of the Spirit that never grows stale, moldy, or rotten, so is the reward for all those who live fruitful and productive lives.

Second, the "crown of exultation" (1 Thess. 2:19–20) is reserved for those who engage in evangelism and discipleship. In the context of 1 Thessalonians, the reward is the joy of knowing that many of the residents of heaven will be there because you and I played a role in their salvation.

As the late William Barclay wrote, "Our greatest glory lies in those whom he has set or helped on the path to Christ."[5]

Third, the "crown of righteousness" (2 Tim. 4:8) is bestowed on those who live obediently in anticipation of the Lord's return. It's not exactly clear what the reward is, but it evidently is a reward based on living obediently while on earth.

Fourth, the "crown of life" (James 1:12; Rev. 2:10) is awarded to those who love the Lord enough to faithfully endure the trials of this life without losing faith or denying Christ—especially enduring to the point of death.

Finally, the "crown of glory" (1 Pet. 5:4) is reserved for those who faithfully and sacrificially serve Christ's church, especially pastors who faithfully teach God's Word and shepherd the congregation God has called them to oversee.

What the "Crowns" Really Mean

"Jesus did not call us to wear a crown in this life," Billy Graham wrote. "He called us to bear a cross and live for Him in the face of ridicule. When we get to Heaven, though, we will put our crosses down and put on the crowns He gives."[6] Nevertheless, some people argue that whatever rewards believers receive in heaven will ultimately be meaningless because we will surrender those rewards to God, as evidenced by the twenty-four elders in Revelation 4:10 (who represent the church in heaven), who "cast their crowns before the throne" in worship to God.

But such a questionable interpretation negates the teaching of the rest of the New Testament that our obedience to God in this life has real consequences in the next life. Instead,

John's vision of this future scene in heaven is a reminder that everything we receive—including our salvation and even our rewards—is ultimately attributable to God's grace, for which we will eternally praise our Creator.

However, that realization does not mean that everyone's experience in heaven will be the same. So what will these "crowns" actually mean to us in heaven? Some believe these rewards are literal crowns we will wear throughout eternity. Others, like myself, believe that although they may be physical crowns (that very well may be cast before the throne of God), they also represent tangible and eternal benefits given to those who have been rewarded by Christ at His judgment seat. These benefits include:

- *Special privileges.* Have you ever been to the "Happiest Place on Earth"? I'm referring of course to Disneyland or Disney World. Amy and I traveled there many times when our girls were young. For a single price you can enter the Magic Kingdom and enjoy the attractions. But for those willing to pay a little more, Disney provides additional benefits: entrance to all the parks, nicer accommodations, and a chance to have breakfast with Mickey and Minnie—or the princesses. In the same way, the Bible teaches that some Christians will enjoy special benefits in heaven: a special welcome by God like a gold medal–winning athlete receiving a ticker-tape parade (2 Pet. 1:11), special access to the tree of life (Rev. 2:7), and even special treatment by Christ Himself (Luke 12:37).
- *Special positions.* We looked at this in some detail in chapter 5, but it bears repeating: those who are faithful on earth will be rewarded with additional responsibilities

in heaven. In the parable of the talents, Jesus commended those who were "faithful with a few things" and rewarded them with the promise to put them "in charge of many things; enter into the joy of your master" (Matt. 25:21).

- *Special praise.* Most of us can recall the joy of hearing a parent say to us, "I'm proud of you." And no one forgets when a boss says, "You're doing a great job. You're an asset to our company." I remember being at the victory party when it was announced that Donald Trump had won the presidency. After his brief speech to his supporters, he walked down to shake hands. When he saw me, he strolled over and said, "Robert, thank you for all you did to make tonight possible. Without you this would not have happened." I will never forget those words! But no praise we receive in this life—even from the most powerful people in the world—will compare to the praise some will receive from Christ in the next life: "Well done, good and faithful servant!" (Matt. 25:21 NIV). That is a reward for which every true believer is striving. Yet it's reserved only for those who are obedient to Christ in this life.

What the Losers Lose at the Judgment Seat of Christ

Some believers will stand before the Lord full of confidence, while others will stand before the Lord full of shame. This is why John warned:

Little children, abide in Him, so that when He appears, we may have confidence and not shrink away from Him in shame at His coming. (1 John 2:28)

187

Those who will blush, hang their heads, and kick the dirt while standing before the judgment seat of Christ will lose what could have been received, which is why John also warned:

> Watch yourselves, that you do not lose what we have accomplished, but that you may receive a full reward. (2 John 8)

Not everyone will experience the same degree of joy and satisfaction in heaven. Those who have built their lives around themselves instead of Christ will experience real, measurable loss. "If any man's work is burned up, *he will suffer loss*," Paul wrote (1 Cor. 3:15). And though his salvation is secure—"he himself will be saved, yet so as through fire"—the loss of heavenly rewards will result in genuine regret.

"But pastor, how can anyone be happy in heaven if they regret lost rewards?" Rejoicing and regret are not mutually exclusive. For example, suppose my insurance agent told me that my house was underinsured by $100,000 and that I should adjust my policy immediately. But instead, I put it off. One night, I awaken to discover my house is engulfed in flames. Groping through the smoke, I throw a chair through a window, and my wife and I barely escape death.

As we stand on the front lawn watching our house being destroyed, what are our emotions? Certainly I'm overjoyed that we escaped the flames and our lives were spared. But that joy is tempered by regret that I didn't make the right financial decision and invest in more insurance.

Many Christians will experience that same mixture of joy and regret at the judgment seat of Christ. While they will be eternally grateful for their escape from the lake of fire, there will also be regret as they watch their lives "go up in smoke" when God judges their works as worthless. And, yes, there will be a sense of loss as they realize the rewards they have forfeited because they invested their lives in the temporal rather than in the eternal.

I can hear some of you saying, "But I thought there would be no sadness in heaven. Doesn't God promise to 'wipe away every tear from our eyes?'" Well, yes and no. It is true that God will "wipe away every tear from their eyes" and that there is no "crying" in the eternal state of the new earth (Rev. 21:4). However, this promise comes *after* the judgment seat of Christ. It makes perfect sense that when we each stand before the Lord's *bema* seat there will be some aspects of our lives burned up in the fire of His holiness. And that loss will cause temporary tears. However, once the Lord has finished His evaluation, whatever tears may have been shed will be gone forever—but the consequences of losing our rewards will endure for eternity.

My former seminary professor and president of Dallas Theological Seminary, the late John Walvoord, encourages us to think about the judgment seat of Christ like a commencement ceremony:

> Some students graduate with honors or high honors, and others receive rewards for distinctive achievements. However, the overwhelming emotion of all the graduates is the joy of receiving the diploma after years of sacrifice and study; every graduate receives a diploma and thus experiences joy and fulfillment. On the one hand, the seriousness of the judgment seat of Christ should be considered; on the other hand, all believers can rejoice in the marvelous grace of God that will enable them all to be in heaven even though they are imperfect in this life.[7]

189

In heaven, there will be real regret for many. But there will be real rejoicing for all. To *underdo* the sadness of losing rewards is to make faithfulness to God in this life irrelevant. However, to *overdo* the sadness of losing rewards is to turn heaven into hell. The goal is to run the race God has set before us, to handle our trust with care, and to build our lives with actions and motives that have eternal value.

In his wonderful book *Your Eternal Reward*, Erwin Lutzer recounts the story of an Indian beggar who crossed paths with a rich rajah riding in a beautiful chariot. The beggar stood by the side of the road, holding out a bowl of rice, hoping for a handout. To his surprise, the rajah stopped and demanded, "Give me some of your rice!" The beggar was angry at the thought that a wealthy man would demand rice from a poor man. But the beggar gave the rajah one grain of rice. "I want more," the rajah demanded. So the beggar gave him another grain. "More rice." By now, the beggar was seething with resentment, but he handed the rajah one more grain of rice.

After the rajah departed, the beggar looked into his bowl of rice. And what he saw astonished him. There, in his bowl, was a grain of gold the size of a grain of rice. He looked more carefully and found two more grains of gold. For every grain of rice he had given, he had received a grain of gold in return.

Lutzer then draws this application: "If we clutch our bowl of rice, we shall lose our reward. If we are faithful and give God each grain, He gives us gold in return. And the gold God gives will survive the fire."[8]

Rice for gold is a pretty savvy trade—but not nearly as lucrative as exchanging temporary pleasures in this life for eternal rewards in that "place called heaven."

9

Who Will Be in Heaven?

I am the way, and the truth, and the life; no one comes to
the Father but through Me.

John 14:6

Maps can be useful in navigating through unfamiliar ter-
ritory. Unfortunately, I had to learn the value of maps the
hard way, some years ago. A pastor friend had invited me to
Canada to speak at his church's annual Valentine's banquet. I
departed Dallas early one morning and, after a plane change
in Minneapolis, landed in Winnipeg, Manitoba, around four
o'clock that afternoon with plenty of time to spare.

After retrieving my luggage, I stood out front waiting
for my host to arrive . . . and waiting . . . and waiting. After
about thirty minutes, I strolled back inside the terminal to
call the pastor's home. When I looked down at the invitation
letter he had mailed a few weeks earlier to retrieve his phone
number, I noticed that the city and province on his letterhead

did not correspond with my present location. Because I had preached for the pastor at his church in Winnipeg ten years earlier, I had assumed he was still at the same church. Big mistake!

I took the letter with me to the airline counter and explained that I had apparently traveled to the wrong city. According to the pastor's letter, I needed to be in Vancouver, British Columbia. Not knowing anything about Canada, I innocently asked, "Is there a bus I can catch to Vancouver? I need to be there in thirty minutes." All the agents behind the counter started laughing and saying in unison, "You've got to be kidding! Vancouver is 1,500 miles west of here!"

Fortunately, a plane was getting ready to depart for Vancouver in the next few minutes. Even though it was a three-hour flight, the two-hour time change between Vancouver and Winnipeg would work in my favor and I could arrive at the church just in time to speak. I ran to the departure gate as fast as possible, and as I was about to walk down the jetway, the gate agent handed me a map of Canada (apparently the story of my mistake had already traveled from the ticket counter to the departure gate). "Here, read this; it might help you the next time you travel to Canada!" she said, and chuckled.

Accidentally traveling to a wrong location can be embarrassing. But there is one time in your life you don't want to end up at the wrong destination—and that's the day of your death. Many will be surprised at the people who will be in heaven. People we may think should be in heaven won't be there, while many people we don't think should be in heaven will be. The worst surprise of all will be for those people who assumed they would be welcomed into God's presence but will instead be turned away from heaven's gate.

The Bible clearly says that only those who have trusted in Christ for the forgiveness of their sins will reside in the new heaven and the new earth. When people argue against the exclusivity of Christ for salvation by saying, "No one but God can decide who will be in heaven," they miss a crucial truth: God has *already* decided the standard by which people will be admitted into His presence. When we declare that faith in Christ offers the only path to heaven, we are not creating our own criterion but simply repeating the requirement God established.

When I suggest that those who are in heaven will surprise us, I'm not at all implying that we will be shocked to see Hindus, Buddhists, and Muslims standing alongside Christians. As I explain in my book *Not All Roads Lead to Heaven*, the popular belief that all religions in the world lead to God negates the most basic teaching of Jesus, who declared, "I am the way, and the truth, and the life; no one comes to the Father but through Me" (John 14:6). The God who never changes is not going to suddenly surprise us by saying at the last minute, "I've changed My mind about this 'faith in Jesus' requirement. Everyone's welcome—come on in!"

What I am saying is that since only God is able to "judge the thoughts and intentions of the heart" (Heb. 4:12), He alone knows who has sincerely placed his or her faith in Christ for the forgiveness of sins. You may be truly surprised by others who are—or are not—in heaven. But, hopefully, you won't be surprised about your *own* eternal fate. If you wait until you have passed from this life into the next life to see whether you are welcomed into God's presence, you will have waited too long.

Unfortunately, many people will be shocked on the judgment day to discover that they will be turned away from heaven's entrance. Jesus described that reality with what I believe are some of the most disturbing words in the entire Bible:

> Not everyone who says to Me, "Lord, Lord," will enter the kingdom of heaven, but he who does the will of My Father who is in heaven will enter. Many will say to Me on that day, "Lord, Lord, did we not prophesy in Your name, and in Your name cast our demons, and in Your name perform many miracles?" And then I will declare to them, "I never knew you; depart from Me, you who practice lawlessness." (Matt. 7:21–23)

Notice it is not just a few people who will be disappointed to discover that they were wrong about their relationship to God. Jesus said "many" who thought they would be welcomed into heaven will instead be dispatched into hell. Why? Simple: they were on the wrong road that led to the wrong destination. Jesus said earlier in Matthew 7 that there were two very different roads or "ways" that led to two very different destinations:

> Enter through the narrow gate; for the gate is wide and the way is broad that leads to destruction, and there are many who enter through it. For the gate is small and the way is narrow that leads to life, and there are few who find it. (vv. 13–14)

How can you make sure you don't make the same tragic mistake? Suppose you live in Oklahoma and want to travel north to Winnipeg, Manitoba, in Canada (on purpose!). You pull your car onto the highway and sincerely believe you are on the right road heading to your intended destination. But several hours into your trip you notice highway signs reading, "Dallas, 100 Miles; Houston, 300 miles." Later on you see a billboard: "Enjoy a night's rest at the Holiday Inn, Laredo, Texas."

Hopefully, those signs would be enough to convince you that you are on the wrong road, heading to the wrong destination. In spite of your sincere belief that you are traveling north, you are, in reality, going south.

The Signposts Leading to Heaven

No one accidentally ends up in heaven or hell without warning. Instead, there are definite "signposts" along the way, alerting us as to whether or not we are on the right path leading to the right destination. The journey to heaven (or hell) begins in this life. If we are truly on the road that leads to heaven, there are four signposts we must acknowledge along the way.

Signpost #1: We Have a Sin Problem

Many people refuse to go beyond this point. They would rather turn around and head another direction than face the unsettling truth of Romans 3:10–12:

> There is none righteous, not even one;
> There is none who understands,

195

There is none who seeks for God;
All have turned aside, together they have become
     useless;
There is none who does good,
There is not even one.

To be "righteous" means to be in a right standing with God. And how many people are naturally in a right relationship with God? Zilch, zero, nada—or as Paul said, "None . . . not even one." We are all sinners. Admittedly, we can always point to those who are worse than we are, such as murderers and child pornographers. We may not be as bad as we *can* be, but we are just as *bad off* as we can be. All of us have sinned, creating an eternal gulf between God and ourselves.

The sin virus we inherited from Adam infects every action, every motive, and every thought. In our honest moments we know that's true. Have you ever been minding your own business—maybe even sitting in church—when some horrible thought comes into your mind? *Where did* that *come from?* you wonder. It's a symptom of the sickness we have all contracted.

Yet even though we experience the symptoms of sin every day, some people still want to claim they are innocent—that the label "sinner" doesn't apply to them. These people are like the little boy who protests to his mother that he has been nowhere near the cookie jar—with crumbs dangling from his chin.

Similarly, we can claim our innocence as vociferously as we want. The problem is that the "cookie crumbs" of sin are all over us, pointing to our guilt. As the apostle John declared:

If we say that we have no sin, we are deceiving ourselves and the truth is not in us [because] if we say that we have not sinned, we make [God] a liar. (1 John 1:8, 10)

Whether we acknowledge it or not, the fact remains: we are all sinners. And the result of sin is death. "The wages of sin is death," Paul wrote in Romans 6:23. As we saw in chapter 7, the Greek word translated "death" is *thanatos*, which means "separation." Just as physical death is the separation of our body from our spirit, spiritual death is the separation of our spirit from God. Physical death is temporary, but spiritual death is eternal. Death is God's righteous judgment on sin. And this leads us to the second signpost.

Signpost #2: God Is Sinless

Since God is the Creator of heaven, He gets to create the rules—not unlike what I used to tell my teenaged girls: "My house, my rules." And the standing rule of heaven is holiness. God's standard demands absolute perfection. No less than six times does God command us, "Be holy because I am holy" (1 Pet. 1:16 NLT).[1]

But we're not holy. And this compounds the problem of sin because it separates us from God. So, how can a sin-infected person ever relate to a sinless God? "Well, God can just overlook our imperfection, can't He?" many ask. "After all, shouldn't God be as tolerant of our sin as we are of other people's sins?" Unfortunately (or fortunately), God is not like we are. The word *holy* literally means "separate." God is "separate" or "different" from humanity. The prophet Habakkuk wrote:

Your eyes are too pure to approve evil,
And You can not look on wickedness with favor.
(Hab. 1:13)

When you couple the reality of this second signpost about God's holiness with the truth of the first signpost about our sinfulness—it's enough to make us very discouraged, very quickly. For example, imagine on your trip from Oklahoma to Winnipeg you see a sign that says, "Winnipeg, 1,300 miles." It's a long trip, but with perseverance you can make it—until you notice your gas gauge indicates only a quarter of a tank left. No problem. You pull into a gas station . . . only to discover you have no cash or credit cards with you. There is a serious deficit between what you have and what you need to get to Winnipeg. At this point you seriously consider doing a U-turn because there is no answer to your dilemma.

The Bible says that to make it to heaven our spiritual "tank" needs to be filled with perfection. The only problem is that none of us has enough goodness to make it all the way to heaven. We may have more than others, but even a tank that is seven-eighths full won't get us there. God demands that our spiritual gas tanks be full and running over if we are going to make it into His presence. So what's the solution? Look at the third signpost.

Signpost #3: Jesus Is the Only Solution to Our Sin Problem

Think back to your imaginary trip to Winnipeg. What if, somewhere in the middle of Kansas, you run out of gas? However, out of nowhere a huge gasoline tanker appears and stops on the road beside you. The driver asks, "What's the problem? Flat tire? Busted radiator?" No, you explain, you just ran out of gas—literally. He grins, points to his rig, and says, "Boy, is this your lucky day! I have more gas in this tanker than you could ever need in your little old car. May I fill your tank for you?"

When Jesus Christ died on the cross for our sins, two amazing transactions took place. First, Jesus—the perfect Son of God who had never sinned—voluntarily accepted the punishment from God we deserve for our sins. Because God is holy, He cannot simply overlook or decide not to punish our sins. Nahum 1:3 declares, "The LORD will by no means leave the guilty unpunished." Someone *has* to pay for our sin—and Jesus volunteered to do just that.

But the second transaction on the cross was even more amazing. God credited us with the righteousness—or perfection—of Jesus. Even though we don't have enough goodness to make it to heaven on our own, Jesus has more than enough and is willing to give us all we need to make up for our deficit. The apostle Paul described these two transactions—Christ getting credited for our sin and us getting credited for Christ's righteousness:

> He [God] made Him [Christ] who knew no sin to be sin on our behalf, so that we might become the righteousness of God in Him. (2 Cor. 5:21)

Jesus is the only Person qualified to bear the punishment for our sins and offer us complete perfection because He's uniquely different from any other person who has ever walked on this planet. He alone is the Son of God. The signpost declaring Jesus to be our sin-substitute is the one that causes many people to stop, stumble, and begin searching for an alternate road to heaven.

In my years of ministry, I have met many sincere, well-meaning, and faithful followers of other religions, including Buddhists, Hindus, Muslims, Jehovah's Witnesses, and Mormons. All of them believed Jesus was a good man, a holy man, a wise man pointing the way to either enlightenment or heaven. But none of them believed His claims to divinity and exclusivity as the *only* means of salvation and way to heaven.[2] C. S. Lewis called such a denial foolish:

> I am trying here to prevent anyone saying the really foolish thing that people often say about Him: "I'm ready to accept Jesus as a great moral teacher, but I don't accept His claim to be God." That is the one thing we must not say. A man who was merely a man and said the sort of things Jesus said would not be a great moral teacher. He would either be a lunatic—on a level with the man who says he is a poached egg—or else he would be the Devil of Hell. You must make your choice. Either this man was, and is, the Son of God: or else a madman or something worse. You can shut Him up for a fool, you can spit on Him and kill Him as a demon; or you can fall at His feet and call Him Lord and God. But let us not come with any patronizing nonsense about His being a great human teacher. He has not left that open to us. He did not intend to.[3]

We must either embrace Jesus's claim that He is God's Son or reject it. There is no intellectually honest alternative, given Jesus's claim that He is the only solution to bridge the gap between our sinfulness and God's holiness: "I am the way, and the truth, and the life; *no one comes to the Father but through Me*" (John 14:6).[4]

Because of the two transactions that took place on the cross—Christ receiving the punishment we deserve and our receiving the righteousness we don't deserve—God offers us entrance into heaven. Paul explained it this way:

Therefore, having been justified by faith, we have peace with God through our Lord Jesus Christ. (Rom. 5:1)

"*Justification*," as my friend Chuck Swindoll defines it, "is God's act of mercy in which He declares believing sinners righteous while they are still in their sinning state."[5] Justification doesn't *make* us righteous, as if we would never sin again. Rather, justification *declares* us righteous, like a judge issuing a pardon to a guilty criminal. Because Jesus took our sins upon Himself and paid for them upon the cross, God forgives us and proclaims us pardoned.

However, God's forgiveness is not a blanket pardon from the penalty of sin for everybody. Instead, justification—God's declaration of "not guilty"—requires faith, just as Paul said: "having been justified by faith." This leads to the final signpost on the road to heaven.

Signpost #4: We Must Choose to Accept Christ's Offer of Forgiveness

If you have made it this far on the narrow road that leads to heaven, you are closer than the vast majority of people who have ever lived. When most people encounter messages declaring them to be guilty before God and deserving of His punishment, they make a U-turn and go the opposite direction. Others who are willing to admit their mistakes still can't come to grips with the idea that Jesus Christ is the only solution to our need for God's forgiveness and start looking for a different path.

However, amazingly, there are some who agree that they are sinners deserving punishment, that God is holy and demanding of complete perfection, and that Jesus is the only solution to their need for God's forgiveness. Yet their response is just to stop where they are and not travel the few steps further to embrace the truth that we must choose to accept Christ's offer of forgiveness.

Think back for a moment to the driver of the gas truck who offers to fill your empty tank so you can make it to your destination: you have a need (gas) and he has the provision for your need (lots of gas). Intellectually agreeing with both of those realities doesn't put one drop of gasoline into your empty tank. You must unscrew the cap on your empty gas tank and receive the gift of the fuel you desperately need.

Similarly, there has to be a point in time when by faith we acknowledge our need for God's forgiveness and accept His offer to allow Christ to pay for our sins and fill us with His perfection. God doesn't force anyone to receive His offer of forgiveness. Only those who choose to receive His gift will be granted entry into heaven.

> But as many as received Him, to them he gave the right to become children of God, even to those who believe in His name. (John 1:12)

This might be a good time to pause and ask where *you* are on the road to heaven. Perhaps you are ready and willing to open your heart to receive God's offer of forgiveness into your life so that you can be sure that one day God will welcome you into His presence. If so, I invite you to take a moment and pray this prayer to God. It's not a magic formula but rather a way to open your heart and receive God's offer of forgiveness.

> *Dear God,*
>
> *Thank You for loving me. I realize that I have failed You in many ways, and I'm truly sorry for the sin in my life. But I believe that You loved me so much that You sent Your Son Jesus to die on the cross for me. I believe that Jesus took the punishment from You that I deserve for my sins. So right now I'm trusting in what Jesus did for me—not my own good works—to save me from my sins. Thank You for forgiving me and helping me to spend the rest of my life serving You. In Jesus's name I pray. Amen.*

If that prayer represents the desire of your heart, you can be assured that you are on the road that leads to heaven. As the apostle John wrote, "These things I have written to you who believe in the name of the Son of God, so that you may know that you have eternal life" (1 John 5:13).

The Inhabitants of Heaven

Jesus was clear that there are only two possible eternal destinations that await us when we die: heaven or hell. He said, "These [the unrighteous] will go away into eternal punishment, but the righteous into eternal life" (Matt. 25:46).

Those who receive God's pardon for their sin by trusting in Jesus Christ are assured of "eternal life" because they are "righteous"—in a right standing with God. Everyone else is guaranteed "eternal punishment" because of his or her refusal to receive God's gracious gift.

What about those who've never had an opportunity to receive Christ's offer of forgiveness? Are they condemned to hell for rejecting an offer they've never heard or were incapable of embracing? Though I deal with this subject extensively in my book *Not All Roads Lead to Heaven*, it might be helpful to briefly discuss the answers to these questions by looking at three groups of people that seem incapable of trusting in Christ for salvation.

The "Heathen" Who Have Never Heard

Christians who hold to the exclusivity of Christ for salvation are often asked about the "heathen" in remote places who haven't heard about Jesus. "How can God send them to hell for rejecting a gospel they've never heard?" they protest. But you don't have to travel to Africa to find people who have never heard about Jesus. Many within our own borders have never heard about Christ, especially as our country becomes increasingly secular. But the question remains: If God is just, how can He condemn people to hell who have not had the opportunity to trust in Christ for salvation?

Paul answers this question in the opening chapters of his letter to the Romans. The apostle affirms that everyone is guilty before God: "For all have sinned and fall short of the glory of God" (Rom. 3:23). In Romans 1–3 Paul declares that those who "fall short" include faithful Jews who observe God's law, moralists who follow their own law, and Gentiles who have never heard about God's law.

In Paul's day, Gentiles were the equivalent of today's "heathen." Gentiles were non-Jews who did not have the benefit of reading the Old Testament or hearing the preaching of the prophets, since they had no relationship with Judaism.

So how could God justly condemn them if they had no opportunity to even know about the one, true God? The answer is that God has provided everyone on the planet enough information to know about God by simply looking at creation:

> For since the creation of the world His invisible attributes, His eternal power and divine nature, have been clearly seen, being understood through what has been made, so that they are without excuse. (Rom. 1:20)

Theologians use the term "natural revelation" to describe information about God that is available to everyone, regardless of whether they have ever read a Bible or heard a sermon. For example, while campaigning in Egypt, the great military leader Napoleon Bonaparte walked the decks of one of his ships anchored in the Mediterranean. One evening he overheard some of his officers mocking the idea of God's existence. The general paused and interrupted. Making a sweeping motion toward the stars, Bonaparte said, "Gentlemen, you must first get rid of these!"

Everyone can look at the world around them and know there is Someone greater than themselves who must have created the universe in which we live. As David exclaimed:

The heavens are telling of the glory of God;
And their expanse is declaring the work of His
   hands.
Day to day pours forth speech,
And night to night reveals knowledge. (Ps. 19:1–2)

Is a belief in the existence of God enough to assure someone entry into this place called heaven? Absolutely not. As
we've seen repeatedly in this book, the New Testament declares that *no one* can be saved apart from exercising faith
in Jesus Christ. So you might wonder, "What use is 'natural
revelation' if it doesn't give people the specific information
about Jesus Christ they need to trust Him for the forgiveness
of sins?" The late theologian Charles Ryrie explained that
natural revelation is not sufficient to save a person, but it is
sufficient—if rejected—to condemn a person.[6]

If the unbeliever who has never heard of Jesus rejects the
"natural revelation" that God has provided about Himself
through creation, Paul says that unbeliever is "without ex-
cuse" (Rom. 1:20). That unbeliever is not only condemned
by his or her own sin but also by his or her refusal to accept
the information about the one true God that nature reveals.

However, if that unbeliever embraces the truth about God
that creation reveals, God will make sure he or she receives
the information about Jesus Christ necessary for salvation.
Remember, God wants to save as many people as possible,
not as few people as possible. The apostle Paul affirms that
God "desires all men to be saved and to come to the knowledge of the truth" (1 Tim. 2:4).

Obviously, not all people *will* be saved. The majority
of humanity will reject God's offer of forgiveness. But the

deepest longing of our heavenly Father is that everyone would respond to His gracious invitation of salvation. However, to be saved one must "come to the knowledge of the truth." And Paul defines that truth in the next two verses of 1 Timothy 2: "For there is one God, and one mediator also between God and men, the man Christ Jesus, who gave Himself as a ransom for all, the testimony given at the proper time" (vv. 5–6).

Doesn't it make sense that if God desires everyone to be saved and that the only way to be saved is by embracing the truth that Jesus Christ died for our sins, then God will ensure that anyone who wants to know God will receive that information about Christ?

A person's response to the natural revelation about God available through creation is a reliable gauge of whether that person truly wants to know God. If the heathen in Africa—or the heathen living next door to you—rejects that knowledge of the true God, then why would he or she respond positively to any more information about Jesus Christ and God's offer of salvation? However, if that person embraces the little information about God he or she receives through creation, we can rest assured that God will provide "the knowledge of the truth" needed for salvation.

The New Testament is filled with illustrations of those who received additional revelation—the special revelation about Jesus Christ necessary for salvation—based on their faith to whatever revelation they had already received. For example, the Roman centurion Cornelius was "a devout man and one who feared God" (Acts 10:2). Cornelius knew nothing about Jesus, but he sincerely wanted to know God. So what did God do? He miraculously orchestrated for the apostle Peter to come to Cornelius's home to share the gospel of Christ. As a result, Cornelius and all of his family were saved and baptized (vv. 44–48).

The same thing happened to an Ethiopian government official who had traveled to Jerusalem to worship the God of Israel. While on his way back to his homeland, the Ethiopian had an encounter with Philip, who had been dispatched by an angel. The Ethiopian was reading from the scroll of Isaiah about the coming Messiah but didn't comprehend what he was reading. So, "Philip opened his mouth, and beginning from this Scripture he preached Jesus to him" (8:35). And the Ethiopian responded, "I believe that Jesus Christ is the Son of God" (v. 37) and was baptized.

I can't tell you the number of times I have received an email or letter from someone saying, "I was flipping through the channels on television and just *happened* across your program, heard about Jesus, and trusted in Him for my salvation." The longer I live the less I believe in mere coincidences. When God sees a man, woman, boy, or girl who truly wants to know Him, He will make sure that person receives the information about Jesus necessary for salvation.

Whenever you are asked about those who have never heard about Jesus Christ, remember this simple truth: no one will ever be condemned to hell for rejecting a gospel they never heard. Instead, those in hell will be there for rejecting the information God has already provided about Himself.

Old Testament Saints Who Lived before Christ

How can we be certain that Adam, Eve, Noah, Sarah, Abraham, Moses, David, Solomon, Rahab, or any of the other Old Testament people we call "saints" are really in heaven? After all, these people lived before Christ's sacrifice on the cross, and God's Word is clear: "There is salvation in no one else; for there is no other name under heaven that has been given among men by which we must be saved" (Acts 4:12). So how can Christ in whom they had never trusted save those who lived before His time?

There is not enough space here to look at each person individually, so let's look at one representative for all those who lived in Old Testament times: Abraham. The average Jew thought of Abraham in the same way the average American thinks of George Washington: he was the "father of the nation"—figuratively and literally! In Genesis 12, God promised to make Abraham the father of the great nation of Israel. Abraham believed God's promise, uprooted his family, and headed toward the land of promise.

Abraham's life was marked by obedience to God: leaving the security of his homeland to head to the Promised Land, allowing his nephew, Lot, to get the best of him in a real estate transaction, and offering to sacrifice his beloved son Isaac to God. If anyone was a candidate for salvation by good works, it was Abraham.

Yet the apostle Paul declared it was Abraham's faith—not his works—that granted him right standing with God:

> If Abraham was justified by works, he has something to boast about, but not before God. For what does the Scripture say? "Abraham believed God, and it was credited to him as righteousness." (Rom. 4:2–3)

Paul's quotation comes from an incident in Abraham's life recorded in Genesis 15, which is key to understanding the apostle's explanation of the source of Abraham's salvation. Abraham had just rescued his nephew Lot from powerful kings in the East. Believing they would retaliate, Abraham feared his family name might come to an end. But then the Lord spoke to Abraham:

> Do not fear, Abram,
> I am a shield to you;
> Your reward shall be very great. (Gen. 15:1)

It looked to Abraham that the promise of Genesis 12—to become the father of a great nation—was about to evaporate. So Abraham wanted to know how the Lord planned to keep His promise: "O Lord God, what will You give me, since I am childless?" (v. 2).

But the Lord wasn't about to renege on the unconditional promise He had made with Abraham. God took him outside and told him to look up and "count the stars" (v. 5). Then God repeated His promise: "So shall your descendants be" (v. 5).

What was Abraham's response? The Bible records that Abraham "believed in the Lord; and He *reckoned* it to him as righteousness" (v. 6). This is the verse Paul quoted two thousand years later in Romans 4:3 to prove that Abraham's salvation was through faith and not through works.

The Hebrew word translated "reckoned" (*chashab*) is an accounting term that means "credited." Think of the faith transaction this way: imagine you go into a store to purchase a new sofa for your living room. The sofa costs $1,000 and you pay with your credit card. Amazingly, by simply allowing the salesperson to swipe that piece of plastic you are allowed to walk out of the store with a valuable piece of furniture. Why would the salesperson allow you to immediately begin experiencing the joy of a new sofa in exchange for a worthless piece of plastic? Although the card itself has no intrinsic value, it represents a promissory note—a promise to pay. Later, when the bill arrives in the mail, it must be paid.

In the same way, when Abraham and others in the Old Testament exercised faith in God, their faith represented a future "promise to pay." Abraham and the other Old Testament believers were immediately "credited" with salvation. And when the bill came due, the only Person capable of satisfying their sin debt paid it. When Jesus cried out on the cross "It is finished" (John 19:30), the word He used was *tetelestai,* a Greek accounting term meaning "paid in full."

Regardless of when a person lives in history, there is only one way anyone can be saved from eternal death—through the payment Jesus Christ made on the cross to satisfy our sin debt. Those who lived before Christ were saved "on credit"—a right standing with God was immediately "reckoned" to their account until Christ could pay their debt on the cross.

Children and the Childlike Who Cannot Believe

As a pastor, one of my most painful duties is ministering to a family that has lost a child, especially if that child was a newborn or infant. One question consumes the thoughts of every family member: "Is my little one in heaven?" Parents and grandparents of deceased teenaged or adult children who are mentally incapacitated to the point of being "childlike" ask this same question: "Are they in heaven?"

211

I wish I could point to one passage of Scripture proclaiming a resounding yes, but I can't. However, we do have the confident claim by one of God's choicest servants, some interesting observations from Jesus's teaching, and the rationale of theology to assure us that children and the childlike do go to heaven when they die.

Just as Abraham serves as an illustration of the faith of all Old Testament saints, so David serves as a representative of all parents who have lost a child before he or she could express faith. David's tragic story began one evening with a rooftop walk. The mighty king of Israel spotted a beautiful woman named Bathsheba bathing in the moonlight. David sent for her and the rest, as they say, is history.

When Bathsheba discovered she was pregnant, David attempted to cover up the fact that he was the father. He recalled Bathsheba's husband, Uriah, from the front lines and tried to convince him to spend the night in his own bed with his wife. Surely, everyone would then surmise that Uriah was the father of his wife's baby. When Uriah refused to indulge in this pleasure out of deference to his fellow soldiers who were still in the field fighting for their country, David arranged to have Uriah murdered, making his death appear to be a battlefield casualty.

Later, the prophet Nathan confronted David over his twin sins of adultery and murder. Instead of continuing the cover-up of his sins, David confessed his transgressions and received God's forgiveness. Nevertheless, God's forgiveness did not erase the temporary—and very painful—consequences of David's actions: a divided kingdom, a disloyal son, and the death of Bathsheba's child.

Immediately after his birth, David and Bathsheba's child became ill and lingered on the edge of death for seven days. During that week, David neither ate nor slept but fasted and prayed for his son's recovery. After the child died, David quickly recovered from his grief and began to eat.

His servants were perplexed. Tradition held that fasting and weeping took place *after* death, not before. Now that the child had died, how could the king go on as if nothing had happened? David's answer was simple and direct—and full of faith. Knowing God would not bring his son back to life, David said: "I will go to him, but he will not return to me" (2 Sam. 12:23).

As long as the child lived, David believed his petitions might move the Lord to heal his son. But once the child died, David knew no amount of fasting and praying would bring his son back. The king could pick himself up and look forward because he believed his son was with God in Paradise. If David believed his son had gone to hell or simply to the grave, he could not have honestly declared that he would see his son again. Instead, the king would have had every reason to continue mourning even more intensely. David's dramatic change in demeanor after his son's death was rooted in the belief that his child had gone to heaven.

Admittedly, David's claim doesn't prove definitively that children and the childlike go to heaven when they die. But if we couple David's claim with some of Jesus's teachings about children, I believe we can make a strong claim that children who die before they are capable of exercising faith in Christ are welcomed into heaven.

For example, in Matthew 18:1–4 Jesus uses a child to illustrate the spiritual quality of humility necessary to receive God's gift of forgiveness:

At that time the disciples came to Jesus and said, "Who then is greatest in the kingdom of heaven?" And He called a child to Himself and set him before them, and said, "Truly I say to you, unless you are converted and become like children, you will not enter the kingdom of heaven. Whoever then humbles himself as this child, he is the greatest in the kingdom of heaven."

Jesus could have selected any child to illustrate the spiritual lesson of humility, but if He had selected one destined for hell then the analogy wouldn't have made sense. The child Jesus selected represented all children—just as Abraham represented Old Testament saints and David's son represented deceased children. By His actions and words, Jesus indicated that all children (and those who are mentally childlike) are destined for heaven.

Beyond the belief of David and the teaching of Jesus, consider the testimony of Scripture. Nowhere in the Bible are children condemned to damnation. Of all the biblical descriptions of hell, infants or little children are never mentioned as residing there. Nor are infants and children described as standing before the great white throne judgment of Revelation 20, which is the precursor to eternal punishment in the lake of fire. I believe this is another piece of evidence that argues strongly for the presence of children in heaven.

Finally, we need to recognize that the Bible distinguishes between inherited sin and the sin of unbelief. As we've seen, humanity—including children—has inherited Adam's guilt and corruption. The fact that everyone—including babies and children—dies is proof that we have all contracted the sickness of sin. Nevertheless, God distinguishes between inherited sin and deliberate sin. He declared that people are responsible for their own sins, not the sins of others:

> The person who sins will die. The son will not bear the punishment for the father's iniquity, nor will the father bear the punishment for the son's iniquity; the righteousness of the righteous will be upon himself, and the wickedness of the wicked will be upon himself. (Ezek. 18:20)

We find a great illustration of the distinction between the guilt of adults and children in Deuteronomy 1. Because of their failure to believe in God's power to give them the Promised Land, God pronounced a sentence of death on the Israelites. They would wander in the wilderness until that unbelieving generation passed away. However, the Lord exempted one group of Israelites from His condemnation. The Lord said:

> Moreover, your little ones who you said would become a prey, and your sons, who this day have no knowledge of good or evil, shall enter there, and I will give it to them and they shall possess it. (Deut. 1:39)

God did not hold the children accountable for the sin of unbelief because they "had no knowledge of good or evil." In the Bible, the sin of unbelief is not simply failing to believe God; it is the deliberate choice not to believe what God has said. Unbelief is the willful rejection of God's revelation—a choice children and the childlike are incapable of making.

Again, none of these arguments is enough in and of itself to say definitively that children and the childlike automatically go to heaven. However, when we consider all of the evidence Scripture provides, I believe we can say that our loving God welcomes children into heaven. As Abraham declared, "Shall not the Judge of all the earth deal justly?" (Gen. 18:25). We can depend upon God to deal justly—and graciously—with those who are incapable of exercising faith in Christ.[7]

Who will be in heaven? It is significant that, outside of those who lived before Christ and children (and the child-like) who are incapable of trusting in Christ, there is no instance in the New Testament of anyone being welcomed into God's presence apart from a personal faith in the Lord Jesus Christ. To attempt to reduce the population of hell by ignoring that requirement and allowing other individuals or groups into heaven is something none of us has the authority to do—especially if we take seriously Jesus's claim that "no one comes to the Father but through [Him]" (John 14:6).

10

How Can I Prepare
for My Journey to Heaven?

Be careful how you walk, not as unwise men but as wise,
making the most of your time, because the days are evil.

Ephesians 5:15–16

When I began this book many months ago, I was preparing to
take an international trip to London. I told you about the list
of things I needed to do to prepare for a journey to a distant,
unfamiliar country—comparing my trip to that journey every
Christian will take one day to that "place called heaven."

My trip ended up being uneventful—except for one mistake: I forgot to pack extra socks. By the third day of the trip
I broke down and bought several pair at a nearby department
store. I knew it was time to do so when my original pair
was standing—instead of lying—at the foot of my bed! My
oversight was inconvenient (and perhaps uncomfortable for

my family members standing downwind from me the first few days), but there was no lasting damage from my lack of preparation.

However, failing to make adequate preparation for our inevitable departure from this life to the next life can have devastating and unending consequences. That is why I want to provide you with a "checklist" of six practical action steps you can take right now to prepare for your journey to heaven.

1. Make Sure You Have a Valid Passport

Making arrangements for your trip to heaven begins with making sure you have the proper "passport" that will allow you into the presence of God. I learned about the importance of passports a number of years ago. When I was a youth minister at the church I now pastor we took our student choir to the Soviet Union. It was during the Cold War and the atmosphere was so oppressive that we couldn't wait to get out of there. Our flight was scheduled to depart at midnight. I watched as our students went through passport control one by one, with obvious expressions of relief on their faces as they passed from bondage to freedom. As the leader, I waited until everyone else was on the other side to pass through myself. I reached inside my coat pocket for my passport—and it was missing.

Panicked, I frantically searched everywhere for the missing document with no success. I explained to the Soviet agent my predicament and that I had to pass through because I was the leader of the group. Trust me, he could not have cared less! No passport, no exit. My wife of exactly one year was standing on the other side crying, imagining her new husband imprisoned in a Russian gulag for the next twenty years!

After watching me sweat for a few minutes, a "friend" of mine appeared waving my passport, which he had taken as a joke. I can assure you that after forty years my wife still doesn't think it's funny. I will never forget the relief I felt as I finally settled in my seat on the plane and winged my way to freedom.

The absolute panic I felt that night more than three decades ago pales in comparison to the terror that will grip the hearts of those who will be denied entrance into heaven because they lack the proper "passport." As they stand at heaven's entrance expecting to be welcomed into God's presence, they will instead hear these words: "I never knew you; depart from Me" (Matt. 7:23).

The people who will be turned away from heaven's gate will not only be atheists and devil worshipers. They will include religious people who consider themselves Christ-followers because of the many good works they performed in the name of Jesus. In fact, they will use their righteous acts as an argument for why they should be allowed into God's presence:

> Many will say to me on that day, "Lord, Lord, did we not prophesy in Your name, and in Your name cast out demons, and in Your name perform many miracles?" (v. 22)

But God will be as unmoved by their pleas as the Soviet guard was by mine. No passport, no entry into heaven.

The only "document" that allows us entry into God's presence for eternity is one that is stamped "Forgiven," and it is given to us the moment we trust in Jesus Christ for our salvation. The theological term for forgiven is *justified*, which means, "to be declared righteous." Our justification before God is not based on our works but on His grace and is received by faith:

> Therefore, having been justified by faith, we have peace with God through our Lord Jesus Christ. (Rom. 5:1)

As we saw in chapter 9, faith in Christ is not just *one* way to heaven—it is the *only* way to heaven.

I realize that to claim Christ as the exclusive way to heaven isn't popular in a world that worships inclusiveness. Many, like billionaire Warren Buffet, believe they can earn their way—or buy their way—into heaven. In 2006, Buffet—the second richest man in the world—announced he was donating 85 percent of his $44 billion fortune to five charitable foundations. "There is more than one way to get to heaven," Buffet declared, "but this is a great way."[1] I commend Buffet on his generosity, but if he persists in believing he can donate his way to salvation, he's in for a rude awakening someday.

How sure are you that at the moment of your death God will welcome you into His presence? Years ago the now-defunct Northwest Airlines offered a promotional gimmick called "The Mystery Fare." For $59 you could purchase a round-trip ticket for a one-day excursion to any city in the continental United States. There was only one catch: you didn't find out where you were heading until you arrived at the airport on the day of the flight. The gimmick worked . . . for a while. Northwest had thousands of customers willing to invest a few bucks and a couple of days to take a chance that they'd end up somewhere exciting, like New York City, Chicago, or Las Vegas.

However, not all customers were happy once they learned of their destinations. One man, who was hoping for a trip to New Orleans, ended up with a ticket to an out-of-the-way city. He walked through the airport terminal bargaining with other "mystery fare" flyers, trying to trade his ticket for another city.

Mystery fares might be a fun chance to take for a one-day adventure, but there is one day in your life you never want to be holding a "mystery fare" ticket: the day of your death. To face eternity without knowing whether you are heading to heaven or hell is a risk no sane person would take. If you wait until the moment you die to discover whether your eternal destination is heaven, you will have waited one second too long. God doesn't want your eternal destiny to be a mystery. That is why the apostle John wrote:

> God has given us eternal life, and this life is in His Son. He who has the Son has life; he who does not have the Son of God does not have life. These things I have written to you *who believe in the name of the Son of God, so that you may know that you have eternal life.* (1 John 5:11–13)

If you do not "know that you have eternal life," why not pause right now and confess to God your need for His forgiveness and express your dependence on Christ's death on the cross for you to save you from the eternal consequences of your sins? When you do that, you can be sure that you have made the most basic preparation necessary for your journey to heaven.

But while that decision is foundational, it is not the only thing you should do to prepare for your journey.

2. Live with a "Destination Mindset"

Trying to live in two places at the same time can be difficult, but it is what every Christian has been called to do—temporarily. Since we don't know when we will suddenly be called away to that "place called heaven," we have to learn how to fulfill our responsibilities in this world while preparing for the next world. Although we are still residents of earth, our "true country" is heaven, as Paul reminded the Philippians: "We are citizens of heaven, where the Lord Jesus Christ lives. And we are eagerly waiting for him to return as our Savior" (Phil. 3:20 NLT). Yet God has charged each of us with responsibilities in this world that involve our work, our families, and especially our ministry for Him as "ambassadors for Christ" (2 Cor. 5:20).

God has called each of us to live with a "here/there" mindset. While living and working here on earth, we are busily preparing for our lives "there" in heaven. Admittedly, it's challenging to live in one location while preparing to live in another place, but it can also be motivating.

I remember when Amy and I were called to the pastorate of my first church in Eastland, Texas, more than thirty years ago. I was serving as a youth minister (at the church I now pastor) but had dreamed of the time I would shepherd my own church. I will never forget that weekend in June 1985 when Amy and I traveled to that small West Texas congregation to "preach in view of a call." After my trial sermon, they ushered us into a small room and fed us pie while the congregation deliberated, debated, and voted. I will never forget the exhilaration I felt when we learned they had voted to call me as their pastor. We could barely sleep that night in our little motel room as we contemplated the adventure before us.

However, the next morning reality set in. We had to drive back to Dallas and spend the next month wrapping up our ministry there. For that month I tried to concentrate on doing the best job I could in Dallas, but my heart was already at my new church ninety miles away. The bulk of my time during that month was devoted to my current responsibilities in Dallas, but some of my energy was devoted to preparing for my new ministry in my new location. Yet I noticed something strange. During that final month in Dallas I had more motivation to work hard than I had experienced during the last seven years—mainly because I knew my time was limited and I wanted to leave things in good shape! Focusing on "there" (my new home in Eastland) profoundly impacted my life "here" (in Dallas).

In the same way, as Christians we have God-given assignments to complete during our brief stay on earth, even though we will soon be departing for our eternal home. Yet while we temporarily reside in this world, we are to guard against becoming entangled in it. Instead, we are to live as "strangers and exiles on the earth" (Heb. 11:13), as we "set [our minds] on the things above" (Col. 3:2).

The great Puritan preacher Jonathan Edwards lived his life with an eternal rather than temporal perspective. Since childhood, Edwards was taught "to think of his own dying, or to live as though he had only an hour left before his death or 'before I should hear the last trump.'"[2] Heaven was so real to Edwards that he wrote:

To go to heaven, fully to enjoy God, is infinitely better than the most pleasant accommodations here. . . . Therefore, it becomes us to spend this life only as a journey toward heaven . . . to which we should subordinate all other concerns of life. Why should we labor for or set our hearts on anything else, but that which is our proper end and true happiness?[3]

Because Edwards chose to live with eternity in mind, when he was nineteen years old he set forth seventy resolutions that guided his life as he prepared for heaven. Here are a few of them:

- "Resolved, to endeavor to obtain for myself as much happiness, in the other world, as I possibly can."
- "Resolved, that I will live so as I shall wish I had done when I come to die."
- "Resolved, to endeavor to my utmost to act as I can think I should do if I had already seen the happiness of heaven and the torments of hell."
- "Resolved, never to do anything I should be afraid of doing if it were the last hour of my life."[4]

As we mentioned in chapter 1, the more seriously we take heaven, the more seriously we'll take earth. Life is short—you don't know when it will be your last day. To be a "heavenly minded" Christian means to live every day as if it were the last day before God calls you home—because someday it will be!

3. Refuse to Allow Death to Paralyze You with Fear

As the departure date for my trip to London approached a few months ago, I experienced a number of emotions: anticipation over visiting a city I had read about, excitement over spending quality time with my family, and urgency to complete my to-do list before I left. But one emotion I never felt was fear. Why should I be afraid of a trip I had planned for and looked forward to for months?

The same principle applies to our journey to heaven. Admittedly, some people—even Christians—are fearful of death. Winston Churchill, who faced death on many occasions during his storied career, feared death's icy grip. He quipped, "Any man who says he is not afraid of death is a liar."[5] One reason Christians are fearful of death is that they are unaware of what awaits them on the other side of it (which is one of the primary reasons I wrote this book). But there are two reasons that Christians do not need to fear death.

First, if you are a Christian you can be assured that you will not depart this earth one second before God's appointed time. That was certainly Paul's conviction. While preaching to the Jews in the synagogue in Antioch, the apostle retraced the history of God's dealing with Israel to prove that the resurrected Jesus was the Messiah. When Paul got to the history of King David, he said, "David, *after* he had served the purpose of God in his own generation, fell asleep, and was laid among his fathers and underwent decay" (Acts 13:36). David didn't die *until* he had served God's purpose during his time on earth. The same is true for us.

"But what about those who die prematurely, such as a teenager in a car accident or a young mother who leaves her small children behind?" you ask. From God's perspective no one dies "prematurely." The psalmist declared, "My times are in Your hand" (Ps. 31:15). God determines our days and numbers our years.

Peter said that Jesus's death occurred according to "the predetermined plan and foreknowledge of God" (Acts 2:23). Just as the day of Jesus's death was determined by God, so is yours. In Ephesians 1:11, Paul wrote that all things in our lives—including death—have been "predestined according to His purpose who works all things after the counsel of His will." No death catches God off guard. He has everything under control. Those who die in faith—whether they are nine or ninety—lived exactly the number of years God prescribed for them. As one person notes, "Every person is immortal until his work on earth is done."

But there is an even more foundational reason Christians don't need to fear death: death is a necessary transition from this world to the next world. Let's stay with our "passport" analogy a moment longer. Once the immigration official has stamped your passport, do you "fear" passing through that little gate that allows you entry into a new country? Of course not—in fact, it's quite an exciting experience, especially if you're leaving the tyranny of the Soviet Union for the freedom of America.

For a Christian, death is nothing more than a transition from an inferior country to a superior one. In fact, without experiencing death we could never travel to that "place called heaven." Paul explains why in 1 Corinthians 15:50:

> Now I say this, brethren, that flesh and blood cannot inherit the kingdom of God; nor does the perishable inherit the imperishable.

Suppose you were traveling from this world to Mars. While your body is perfectly suited for the earth's atmosphere, it is totally unsuitable for the "red planet" (or any other planet). Similarly, our present body of "flesh and blood" is specifically designed for life in this world but could never function in the next world. That is why there must be a time when we are separated from our earthly body. As I've noted before, the word *death* comes from the Greek word *thanatos*, or "separation." Death is a necessary separation from our earthly body so we can put on our new body.

Here's another way of thinking about death. Imagine you were invited to a presidential inauguration ball like Amy and I once attended. Men, on the morning of the event would you object to exchanging your pajamas for a Brioni suit? Ladies, would you resist taking off your bathrobe and putting on a Chanel dress? I don't think so! God has invited every Christian to a magnificent location for which we must be properly dressed, and He has provided the appropriate "wardrobe." Death is nothing more than exchanging inferior clothing for superior clothing.

Randy Alcorn, in his book *Heaven*, employs yet another metaphor to describe death: a surprise party.[6] Suppose a friend invites you to a party where you will know some people but not many. The food is adequate but nothing extraordinary. You enjoy meeting some new people and visiting with the few familiar people you know. Suddenly your friend announces it's time to leave. Although you're not quite ready to leave, you acquiesce because he's your ride home.

When your friend drops you off at your house, you place your key in the lock and turn the knob. Just as you open the door the lights suddenly come on. "Surprise!" Your family and your closest friends are there. They've brought gifts and have covered your table with your favorite delicacies. The first party was simply a ruse to get you out of the house so that the second party could be organized. Had you stayed at the first party, you would have missed the real party—the one at your home.

Life on earth is like the first party—pleasant enough. But at death you open the doors to your true home and discover that the real party is taking place there.

I wish I could tell you that every Christian I know who learned he or she was terminally ill faced their death with great anticipation and no fear. But that wouldn't be honest. Through the years, some believers I have talked with who were facing the end of their life expressed regret about "leaving the party too soon" even though they had great faith about their future home in heaven. They were sad over what they might be missing on earth.

However, the real party is already underway in heaven! Any sadness Christians feel over leaving this earth will be more than compensated for with the hilarity of heaven. I believe this is what Jesus had in mind when He promised, "Blessed [literally, "Happy"] are you who weep now, for you shall laugh" (Luke 6:21).

4. Make the Most of Your Time on Earth

Though Moses beat today's average life span by forty or fifty years—dying at 120—his admonition about the value and brevity of life is worth heeding:

> Seventy years are given us! And some may even live to eighty. But even the best of these years are often empty and filled with pain; soon they disappear, and we are gone. . . . Teach

us to number our days and recognize how few they are; help us to spend them as we should. (Ps. 90:10, 12 TLB)

I'll never forget the first time I heard someone speak on these verses. I was a freshman in college at Baylor University sitting in an orientation chapel, pining for my girlfriend (now my wife) who was one hundred miles away at the University of Texas. It would be two weeks until I saw her, and Moses's observation about the brevity of time seemed profoundly untrue. Time moved like molasses back then! Yet, the older I get the more I understand what Moses was saying. As one wag put it, "Life is like a roll of toilet paper—the closer you get to the end, the more quickly it goes."

The apostle Paul picked up and expanded on Moses's idea of numbering our days and learning to live wisely:

Be careful how you walk, not as unwise men but as wise, making the most of your time, because the days are evil. (Eph. 5:15–16)

"Walking" in the Bible is a metaphor for living. And whatever consumes your time determines "how you walk"—the way you live. For example, try this simple exercise: make a list of your top three priorities in life. Then, over the next few days, track how much of your time you actually spend on these three priorities. Are you "walking"—spending your time—on those things you deem most important in your life? As one person has said, "Life is like a dollar. You can spend it any way you want, but you can only spend it once."

Paul admonished us to live wisely by "making the most of [our] time" (v. 16). Literally, that phrase means to "buy

229

up" the time. In other words, invest in life and take hold of it—seize the day, *carpe diem*. Philosopher Henry David Thoreau feared that when his death-day came he would "discover that [he] had not lived." He wrote, "I did not wish to live what was not life. . . . I wanted to live deep and suck out all the marrow of life . . . to put to rout all that was not life, to cut a broad swath and shave close."[7] Simply put: don't waste time—life is too short and precious for that.

Spending hours watching television, playing video games, or scrolling through Facebook and Twitter would have been unthinkable to Thoreau and Paul. For both men, life was too valuable a commodity to waste. Thoreau believed he could "buy up" life by secluding himself in the woods, "to live deliberately, to front only the essential facts of life, and see if I could not learn what it had to teach."[8]

Paul had a different motivation for "making the most of [the] time." He saw "the days [as] evil" (v. 16). Make no mistake: Satan will do whatever it takes to prevent you from living a purposeful and God-honoring life. Satan will entice you to squander your time (and therefore your life) on worthless pursuits rather than your God-given priorities in life. I think the paraphrase by J. B. Phillips best captures what Paul had in mind about making the most of your brief time on earth:

> Live life, then, with a due sense of responsibility, not as men who do not know the meaning and purpose of life but as those who do. Make the best use of your time, despite all the difficulties of these days. Don't be vague but firmly grasp what you know to be the will of God. (Eph. 5:15–17)

5. Minimize Your "Predeparture" Regrets

Have you ever been at the departure gate at an airport about to board a plane when you think *I should have remembered to stop the newspaper*, or *I wish I had remembered to pack a warmer coat*? Such "predeparture" regrets are real, but they are also trivial compared to the deep regrets many people feel as they prepare to leave this world for the next one. In my position as a pastor, few things are more heartbreaking than to sit at the deathbed of someone consumed with regrets, hearing them weep over the things they wished they had said—or not said—to their loved ones or over the things they wished they had done or not done in life.

Nothing will steal your joy faster or devour your days more completely than regrets. Poet John Greenleaf Whittier captured this mournful emotion with these lines:

> For all sad words of tongue or pen,
> The saddest are these: "It might have been."[9]

Working in a palliative care center, author Bronnie Ware heard many deathbed confessions, and was able to create a list of the top five regrets of the dying:

1. "I wish I'd had the courage to live a life true to myself, not the life others expected of me."
2. "I wish I hadn't worked so hard."
3. "I wish I'd had the courage to express my feelings."
4. "I wish I had stayed in touch with my family."
5. "I wish I had let myself be happier."[10]

Regrets are like cancer. They eat away at your soul, consume your peace of mind, and are no way to spend your days preparing for heaven. My father was a successful man by any standard. He was a follower of Christ, held an important position in the airline industry, enjoyed an upper-middle-class income, traveled the world, was respected by colleagues and friends, and was loved by his family.

Yet during the months preceding his death from pancreatic cancer, I listened to him lament over the "what ifs" and "if onlys" of his life: trips he wished he had taken, career opportunities he didn't maximize, words he should never have spoken, and relationships he didn't fully appreciate. He even regretted not wearing new suits he had purchased for fear of "wearing them out."

My dad's final months on this earth were not altogether happy ones. Through his experience I learned that regrets have the power to extinguish the joy of an otherwise happy life. I also learned that in the end, someone else is either going to sell or give away your clothes—just as we did with my dad's suits—so you might as well wear them today.

As you prepare for your journey to that "place called heaven," one of the best resolutions you can make is to rid your life of any unnecessary regrets. One way to do this is to honestly evaluate your life. Take a sheet of paper and divide it into five columns: God, family, friends, career, and finances (it might look something like the chart below). Under each column write three goals you'd like to achieve in each of these life areas before you die.

God	Family	Friends	Career	Finances

If it helps, think back to Jonathan Edwards's list and write your goals as resolutions. For example:

- Resolved: I will glorify God so I might hear Him say, "Well done, good and faithful servant."
- Resolved: I will appreciate, enjoy, and value the mate God has given me.
- Resolved: I will endeavor to point my children to Christ, to earn their respect, and to celebrate their uniqueness.
- Resolved: I will treasure my friendships by praying for and spending time with those who enrich my life.
- Resolved: I will choose a lifework that utilizes my giftedness and passions, and will strive to provide a stable financial foundation for my family both now and in the future.
- Resolved: I will make sure that my finances are in order and my family is provided for when I die.
- Resolved: I will ask forgiveness from anyone I have wronged so that when I'm gone they will always remember I tried to make things right.

As you honestly evaluate your life, maybe you feel badly about mistakes you've made, opportunities you've squandered, or people you've hurt. The truth is that it is impossible to erase the past. Life has no rewind button. But with God's help you can make some changes in your life right now that will reshape your tomorrow and your eternity. If you don't believe that, consider the story of one Swedish philanthropist.

Alfred Nobel was a nineteenth-century chemist who made his reputation and fortune by stabilizing nitroglycerine. By adding a specific compound to the highly volatile liquid, Nobel was able to turn it into a paste, which he called "dynamite." Intended for commercial construction—blasting mines, drilling tunnels, and building canals—dynamite was quickly adapted by governments into an instrument of war.

During his lifetime, Nobel was best known as the inventor of dynamite—and for the death and destruction it caused. In fact, when his brother Ludvig died in 1888, French newspapers confused Ludvig for Alfred and reported, "The merchant of death is dead." This mistake meant that Alfred Nobel had the opportunity to read his own obituary in the newspaper.

Realizing that when he died he would only be remembered for enabling the killing of untold millions of people, Nobel decided right then to make a significant change in his life. He determined to dedicate the remainder of his life to scientific, artistic, and peaceful endeavors that celebrated humanity. He set aside a sizable sum of his vast wealth and established the Nobel prizes we're familiar with today.

Few of us will achieve the fame and fortune of Alfred Nobel, but all of us can redirect our time, our money, and our energy to things that will allow us to live and die without regrets.

6. Take Care of the Practical Matters before You Depart

One last item to check off before departing on your heavenly journey: make sure those you leave behind will be adequately cared for. That's what the prophet Isaiah told King Hezekiah: "Thus says the LORD, 'Set your house in order, for you shall die'" (2 Kings 20:1). Good advice.

A friend of mine attended a seminar about the need to make adequate financial preparations for families in the event of the death of a husband or wife. My friend returned from the conference convicted that he needed to have a frank talk with his wife about what she should do if he preceded her in death. "Honey, I think you should plan to stay in the house since the mortgage is almost paid," he said. She agreed. "And if you choose to remarry, that's fine with me. In fact, I would have no problem with your new husband and you occupying our bedroom." Again, no disagreement from his wife.

"And also, I would want him to feel free to use my golf clubs if he was as passionate about the game as I am," he added. "Oh, no! That would never work!" my friend's wife said. "Why not?" her husband wondered. "Because you're right-handed and he's left-handed!"

Funny story. But what isn't humorous is a scenario I've seen played out far too many times: a spouse dies without ever discussing financial affairs, the location of his or her will or life insurance policies (if either exist), security passwords, funeral desires, or any other vital information with the surviving spouse or children. The result is that the family is completely in the dark about critical issues, leading them to waste energy and time that should be directed toward grieving and recovery.

I've said it before in this book and I'll say it again: death is inevitable. You are going to die and leave your family behind. As popular speaker Tony Campolo notes, one day your family and friends will cart your casket to the cemetery, drop you in a hole, throw dirt on you, and go back to the church and eat potato salad. But what will your family do after the potato salad?

One thing you could do is follow the example of Jim Hindle, a Certified Financial Planner. A few years before his death, Jim wrote an article on how to leave your financial house in good order. Jim based his advice on 1 Timothy 5:8: "If anyone does not provide for his own, and especially for those of his household, he has denied the faith and is worse than an unbeliever."

Besides having a will, Jim advised, families should create a notebook, listing assets and liabilities, checking and savings accounts, stocks, bonds, CDs, IRAs, pensions, real estate, life insurance policies, and annuities. The notebook should also include obituary information as well as contact information for an attorney, accountant, banker, and stockbroker.

A few days after Jim's death, still reeling with the new reality of his passing, his wife, Audrey, went to see her attorney—Jim's notebook in hand. "After looking at the book," she writes, "he shook his head and said, 'This is incredible.'" She concludes:

> Jim demonstrated love, godly character, and integrity by leaving a part of himself in his book. I have never felt abandoned or insecure. My husband took good care of us in his life, and is still taking care of us in his death.[11]

Do that for your family. You won't regret it . . . and neither will they.

The early death of both of my parents had a profound effect on my life. Both were strong believers who taught me not only how to live as a Christian but also how to die as a Christian. But their premature deaths (at least from my perspective) steeled my resolve to live without regrets and to die without regrets.

If I were to compose my own epitaph to be engraved on my headstone, I couldn't come up with anything better than the one engraved on Abraham's headstone: "[He] died in a ripe old age, an old man and satisfied with life; and he was gathered to his people" (Gen. 25:8). Abraham came to the end of his life without a long list of "if onlys" or "what ifs." He was satisfied—contented—with his past. By faith in God's grace he knew his past mistakes had been forgiven. He was satisfied, knowing that he had passed along his faith in God to his children and grandchildren. And he was at peace with the future—prepared for his journey to heaven where he would be "gathered to his people."

Are you ready for your journey to heaven? If you are a Christian, you need not fear the journey—especially when you consider the destination. One of the most moving illustrations of the journey and destination that await every Christian was penned many years ago by John Todd. Born in Rutland, Vermont, in the autumn of 1800, John moved with his family to the tiny hamlet of Killingsworth. A few years later, young John was orphaned when his mother and father died. His siblings were parceled out to family members—and a kindhearted aunt agreed to take in six-year-old John.

John lived with his aunt for fifteen years, then in his early twenties he left to study for the ministry. As the years passed and John reached midlife, his aunt fell ill. Realizing death was close, she wrote to her nephew. She was frightened about the prospect of dying. Moved with compassion, John responded, recounting the night when he, a frightened little boy, was welcomed into the warm and loving home of his aunt:

It is now thirty-five years since I, a little boy of six, was left quite alone in the world. You sent me word you would give me a home and be a kind mother to me. I have never forgotten the day when I made the long journey of ten miles to your house in North Killingsworth. I can still recall my disappointment when, instead of coming for me yourself, you sent your colored man, Caesar, to fetch me. I well remember my tears and my anxiety as, perched high on your horse and clinging tight to Caesar, I rode off to my new home. Night fell before we finished the journey, and as it grew dark I became lonely and afraid.

"Do you think she'll go to bed before I get there?" I asked Caesar anxiously. "O no," he said reassuringly. "She'll sure stay up FOR YOU. When we get out of these here woods you'll see her candle shining in the window." Presently we did ride out in the clearing and there, sure enough, was your candle. I remember you were waiting at the door, that you put your arms close about me and that you lifted me—a tired and bewildered little boy—down from that horse. You had a big fire burning on the hearth, a hot supper waiting for me on the stove. After supper, you took me to my new room, you heard me say my prayers and then you sat beside me until I fell asleep.

You probably realize why I am recalling all this to your memory. Someday soon, God will send for you, to take you to a new home. Don't fear the summons—the strange journey— or the dark messenger of death. God can be trusted to do as much for you as you were kind enough to do for me so many years ago. At the end of the road you will find love and a welcome waiting, and you will be safe in God's care.[12]

A Final Thought

Heaven is the destination that awaits all those who love the Lord Jesus Christ. And it is more glorious than mere words can begin to describe. Not long ago I attended a stage production of the classic musical *The Sound of Music*. The Rogers and Hammerstein score is timeless and the actors were superb. But when the curtain rose for the opening act, I had to keep myself from laughing out loud.

There was the young nun Maria singing and frolicking in front of a painted scrim depicting the Austrian Alps. A few months earlier I had been in the Alps visiting the actual locations where the movie was filmed. The disparity between those real majestic mountains and the artistic rendering on a piece of fabric was laughable.

I've thought about that disparity over the last six months as I have written this book. The words on these pages—or even the pages of Scripture itself—are only a pencil sketch of that very real location Jesus is preparing for you right now.

It's a place more magnificent than you could ever imagine.

It's a place where every heartache will be erased and every dream will be fulfilled.

It's a place reserved for those who have received God's forgiveness through faith in Christ.

It's a place called heaven.

Notes

Chapter 1 What Difference Does a Future Heaven Make in My Life Today?

1. Philip Yancey, *Disappointment with God: Three Questions No One Asks Aloud* (Grand Rapids: Zondervan, 1988), 276.

2. Author unknown, as quoted in Robert Jeffress, *How Can I Know: Answers to Life's 7 Most Important Questions* (Brentwood, TN: Worthy Publishers, 2012), 137.

3. Joni Eareckson Tada, *Heaven: Your Real Home* (Grand Rapids: Zondervan, 1995), 15.

4. Ibid., 110.

5. William Shakespeare, *Hamlet*, 3.1.79, in *William Shakespeare: The Complete Works* (New York: Dorset Press, 1988), 688.

6. C. S. Lewis, *Mere Christianity* (San Francisco: HarperSanFrancisco, 2001), 134.

7. Spiros Zodhiates, *What You Should Know about Life After Death* (Chattanooga, TN: AMG, 2002), 49.

8. Cyprian, "Treatise VII: On the Mortality," 26, in *The Ante-Nicene Fathers*, vol. 5, ed. Alexander Roberts and James Donaldson (New York: Charles Scribner's Sons, 1903), 475.

9. Aristides, "The Apology of Aristides on Behalf of the Christians," 15, trans. J. Rendel Harris, *Texts and Studies: Contributions to Biblical and Patristic Literature*, vol. 1, no. 1, ed. J. Armitage Robinson (London: Cambridge at the University Press, 1893), 49.

10. John Charles Ryle, *Shall We Know One Another and Other Papers* (Moscow, ID: Charles Nolan Publishers, 2001), 5–6.

11. The third heaven referred to by Paul in 2 Corinthians 12:2 is the place of God's presence—"Paradise" (12:4; see Deut. 26:15; Ps. 14:2; Matt. 6:9–10; 18:18; 28:2). The first heaven is the earth's atmosphere (Gen. 1:20, 26, 28; 8:2; Deut. 28:12; Job 35:5; Ps. 147:8; Matt. 8:20; 13:32; 16:2–3). The second heaven is the stellar universe, the place of stars and planets (Gen. 1:14–15, 17; 15:5; Deut. 4:19; 17:3; 28:62; Acts 2:19–20; Heb. 11:12).

12. "Hell Unleashed," *Gladiator*, directed by Ridley Scott (2000; Universal City, CA: Universal Studies, 2004), DVD.

13. Lucius Annaeus Seneca, "Consolations Against Death from the Providence and Necessity of It," in *Seneca's Morals by Way of Abstract*, trans. Roger L'Estrange (London: Sherwood, Neely and Jones, 1818), 237.

14. C. S. Lewis, *The Last Battle*, in *The Complete Chronicles of Narnia* (New York: HarperCollins, 1998), 524 (emphasis in original).

15. See Randy Alcorn, *Heaven* (Carol Stream, IL: Tyndale, 2004), 436.

16. Bruce Wilkinson and David Kopp, *A Life God Rewards: Why Everything You Do Today Matters Forever* (Colorado Springs: Multnomah, 2002), 16.

17. Alcorn, *Heaven*, 471.

18. Teresa of Avila, as quoted in Lee Strobel, *The Case for Faith: A Journalist Investigates the Toughest Objections to Christianity* (Grand Rapids: Zondervan, 2000), 65.

19. Alcorn, *Heaven*, 460.

Chapter 2 Is Heaven a Real Place or Is It a State of Mind?

1. David Jeremiah, *Answers to Your Questions about Heaven* (Carol Stream, IL: Tyndale, 2013), 3.

2. "Heaven," *The Merriam-Webster Dictionary* (Springfield: Merriam-Webster, 2005).

3. See Luke 10:1 and John 11:48.

4. The Vulgate—the Latin version of the Bible—translates the noun *mone*, "dwelling," as *mansiones*. The King James or Authorized Version transliterates this into "mansions." However, the point of Jesus's teaching in John 14:2 is not that believers will live in their own individual mansions but that we will live in God's mansion and be given keys to our own individual rooms. The idea comes from the marriage custom of Jesus's day. The bridegroom would retrieve his bride from her home and bring her back to his father's house, where an apartment was built for the new couple.

5. On Jesus being the only means of reaching heaven, please see my book *Not All Roads Lead to Heaven: Sharing an Exclusive Jesus in an Inclusive World* (Grand Rapids: Baker, 2016).

6. If you are unfamiliar with end-time events, please see my book *Perfect Ending: Why Your Eternal Future Matters Today* (Brentwood, TN: Worthy, 2014).

7. Other biblical passages that speak of the passing of the present heavens and earth include Psalm 102:25–26, Isaiah 51:6, and Matthew 24:35.

8. See Ron Rhodes, *The Wonder of Heaven: A Biblical Tour of Our Eternal Home* (Eugene, OR: Harvest House, 2009), 135.

9. See Jeremiah, *Answers to Your Questions about Heaven*, 115.

10. We believe the New Jerusalem is cube-shaped (as opposed to, for example, pyramid-shaped) because the Holy of Holies, God's dwelling place in Solomon's temple, was cube-shaped (1 Kings 6:20).

11. Sam Roberts, "It's Still a Big City, Just Not Quite So Big," *New York Times*, May 22, 2008, http://www.nytimes.com/2008/05/22/nyregion/22shrink.html.

12. Ron Rhodes, *What Happens After Life? 21 Amazing Revelations about Heaven and Hell* (Eugene, OR: Harvest House, 2014), 69.

13. Exactly why twelve angels are stationed at the twelve gates, which are inscribed with the twelve tribes of Israel, and why the twelve foundations are inscribed with the twelve apostles, is a mystery. See Rhodes, *What Happens After Life?*, 70–71.

14. The Greek word for "healing" in Revelation 22:2 is *therapeia*, from which we get the English word *therapy*. The basic idea of *therapeia* is "health giving." Since there will be no sickness or death in heaven (21:4), it's best to interpret the word as the promotion of well-being. Notice, however, there's no mention of the tree of the knowledge of good and evil. There's no need to test humanity in heaven. The redeemed already know of sin and its devastating effects and have been saved by the blood of Christ, who passed the test; they desire it no longer.

15. C. S. Lewis, *The Problem of Pain*, in *The Complete C. S. Lewis Signature Classics* (New York: HarperCollins, 2002), 428.

Chapter 3 Have Some People Already Visited Heaven?

1. "Dwight L. Moody Is Dead," *New York Times*, December 23, 1899, http://query.nytimes.com/mem/archive-free/pdf?res=9B04E1DA153CE433A25750C2A9649D94689ED7CF.

2. "Near-Death Experiences: Key Facts," International Association for Near-Death Studies, accessed January 12, 2017, https://iands.org/images/stories/pdf_downloads/Key%20Facts%20Handout-brochure-small.pdf.

3. Gideon Lichfield, "The Science of Near-Death Experiences," *Atlantic*, April 2015, http://www.theatlantic.com/features/archive/2015/03/the-science-of-near-death-experiences/386231/.

4. "'Heaven Is for Real' Hit Major Sales Milestone," *Christian Retailing*, December 11, 2014, https://web.archive.org/web/20141218031545/http://christianretailing.com/index.php/newsletter/latest/27680-heaven-is-for-real-hits-major-sales-milestone.

5. Alex Malarkey, as quoted in Dustin Germain, "'The Boy Who Came Back from Heaven' Recants Story, Rebukes Christian Retailers," *Pulpit & Pen* (blog), January 13, 2015, http://pulpitandpen.org/2015/01/13/the-boy -who-came-back-from-heaven-recants-story-rebukes-christian-retailers/.

6. Tyndale House Publishers' press release, as quoted in Ron Charles, "'The Boy Who Came Back from Heaven' Actually Didn't; Books Recalled," *Washington Post*, January 16, 2015, https://www.washingtonpost .com/news/style-blog/wp/2015/01/15/boy-who-came-back-from-heaven -going-back-to-publisher/.

7. Malarkey, as quoted in Germain, "'The Boy Who Came Back from Heaven' Recants Story."

8. J. Isamu Yamamoto, "The Near-Death Experience, Part Two: Alternative Explanations," *Christian Research Journal*, Summer 1992, http:// www.iclnet.org/pub/resources/text/cri/cri-jrnl/web/crj0098a.html.

9. "Miracle Makers," *The Princess Bride*, directed by Rob Reiner (1987; Beverly Hills, CA: MGM Studios, 1999), DVD.

10. On Colton Burpo's descriptions of the Holy Spirit and God the Father, see "Frequently Asked Questions," Heaven Is for Real Ministries, http://www.heavenlive.org/about/faq.

11. Yamamoto, "The Near-Death Experience, Part Two: Alternative Explanations."

12. Dinesh D'Souza, *Life After Death: The Evidence* (Washington, DC: Regnery, 2009), 68.

13. Lichfield, "Science of Near-Death Experiences."

14. See Deuteronomy 18:10–13; Galatians 5:19–21; and Revelation 21:8.

15. See Rhodes, *Wonder of Heaven*, 241.

Chapter 4 Do Christians Immediately Go to Heaven When They Die?

1. Reinhold Niebuhr, as quoted in David L. Chappell, *A Stone of Hope: Prophetic Religion and the Death of Jim Crow* (Chapel Hill: University of North Carolina Press, 2004), 50.

2. Alcorn, *Heaven*, xix.

3. J. Sidlow Baxter, *The Other Side of Death: What the Bible Teaches About Heaven and Hell* (Grand Rapids: Kregel Publications, 1987), 22.

4. Jack Nicholson, as quoted in Rhodes, *Wonder of Heaven*, 26–27.

5. Tada, *Heaven: Your Real Home*, 201.

6. As quoted in Rhodes, *Wonder of Heaven*, 48.

7. Alcorn, *Heaven*, 57.

8. Charles Dickens, *A Christmas Carol* (New York: Barnes & Noble, 2005), 17.

9. Erwin W. Lutzer, *How You Can Be Sure You Will Spend Eternity with God* (Chicago: Moody Publishers, 2015), 9.

Chapter 5 What Will We Do in Heaven?

1. Mark Twain, as quoted in Archibald Henderson, *Mark Twain* (New York: Frederick A. Stokes Co., 1912), 109.

2. Mark Twain, "Tammany and Croker," in *Mark Twain's Speeches* (New York: Harper & Brothers Publishers, 1910), 117.

3. Isaac Asimov, as quoted in Alcorn, *Heaven*, 409.

4. G. K. Chesterton, *Orthodoxy* (Wheaton, IL: Harold Shaw Publishers, 1994), 61.

5. See Katy Sharp, "A Tour of the NFL's Loudest Stadiums," *SB Nation*, September 18, 2014, http://www.sbnation.com/nfl/2014/9/18/6257281/nfl-loudest-stadiums; and Kevin Lynch, "Seattle Seahawks Fans 'Cause Minor Earthquake' with World Record Crowd Roar," *Guinness World Records*, December 4, 2013, http://www.guinnessworldrecords.com/news/2013/12/seattle-seahawks-fans-cause-minor-earthquake-with-world-record-crowd-roar-53285/.

6. Tada, *Heaven: Your Real Home*, 64.

7. Alcorn, *Heaven*, 196.

8. See Luke 22:69; Acts 2:33; 7:55–56; Romans 8:34; Ephesians 1:20; Colossians 3:1; Hebrews 1:3; 8:1; 10:12; 12:2; 1 Peter 3:22; Revelation 3:21.

9. For more information on the millennial kingdom, see my book *Perfect Ending: Why Your Eternal Future Matters Today* (Brentwood, TN: Worthy Publishing, 2014), 137–60.

10. Jeremiah, *Answers to Your Questions about Heaven*, 32.

11. Sam Storms, as quoted in Alcorn, *Heaven*, 179.

Chapter 6 Do People in Heaven Know What Is Happening on Earth?

1. Though the Bible often refers to the body sleeping as a metaphor for death (John 11:11–14; Acts 7:59–60; 13:36; 1 Thess. 4:13), nowhere does the Bible speak of soul sleep. The Greek word translated "to fall asleep" is *koimao*, which comes from the same Greek word translated "to lie down." *Koimao* was used to describe someone who slept in a hotel

for the night and in the morning continued his journey. This is what happens to the believer's body at death. The body "sleeps" in the ground, while the soul gets up and continues its journey to heaven. See Jeremiah, *Answers to Your Questions about Heaven*, 12.

2. Warren Wiersbe, *The Wiersbe Bible Commentary: New Testament* (Colorado Springs, CO: David C. Cook, 2007), 1097.

3. See Joshua 15:8; 18:16; 2 Kings 23:10; Nehemiah 11:30.

4. See 2 Chronicles 28:3; 33:6; Jeremiah 19:6; 32:35.

5. C. S. Lewis, *The Screwtape Letters* (San Francisco: HarperSanFrancisco, 2001), 61.

6. See Matthew 7:13; 2 Thessalonians 1:8–9; see also 1 Corinthians 5:5; 1 Thessalonians 5:3; 1 Timothy 6:9.

7. On our endless worship of God see Revelation 1:6; 4:9; and 5:13. On the endless life of God see Revelation 4:10 and 10:6. And on the endless kingdom of God see Revelation 11:15.

8. James Joyce, *A Portrait of the Artist as a Young Man* (New York: Everyman's Library, 1991), 151–52.

9. Peter Kreeft, *Christianity for Modern Pagans: Pascal's Pensées* (San Francisco: Ignatius Press, 1993), 196.

10. Randal Rauser, as quoted in Rhodes, *Wonder of Heaven*, 144.

11. J. I. Packer, *Knowing God* (Downers Grove, IL: InterVarsity Press, 1973), 138.

12. J. I. Packer, "Hell's Final Enigma," *Christianity Today* 46, no. 5 (April 22, 2002): 84, http://www.christianitytoday.com/ct/2002/april22 /27.84.html.

Chapter 7 Will We Know One Another in Heaven?

1. Erma Bombeck, as quoted in Charles R. Swindoll, *Improving Your Serve: The Art of Unselfish Living* (Nashville: W Publishing Group, 1981), 51.

2. Chart copyright © 1979, 2008, 2017 by Charles R. Swindoll, Inc. All rights reserved. Used by permission. The "Millennial Believer" section is not part of the original chart, and the opinions expressed in this section are the author's own and do not necessarily reflect the view of Charles R. Swindoll, Inc. or Insight for Living Ministries.

3. John Calvin, as quoted in Rhodes, *Wonder of Heaven*, 84.

4. See 1 Corinthians 15:12–19.

5. Luke 24:33 mentions that the two Emmaus disciples found the eleven disciples. However, since Thomas was absent at the time, the term "the eleven" is used in a technical sense to indicate the disciples as a whole.

6. Tada, *Heaven: Your Real Home*, 53.

7. Revelation 5:9 and 7:9 tell us that heaven is populated by people from every nation, tribe, and tongue, leading me to believe that we'll keep our racial distinctions in heaven.

8. Alcorn, *Heaven*, 290 (emphasis in original).

9. Ibid., 287.

10. Rhodes, *What Happens After Life?*, 107.

Chapter 8 Will Heaven Be the Same for Everyone?

1. See Ephesians 6:8; Revelation 2:23; Matthew 12:36–37; Luke 19:11–26; 1 Peter 1:17; Matthew 10:41–42; Luke 14:12–14; Luke 6:27–28, 35; Daniel 12:3; and Matthew 6:1–4 respectively.

2. Paul doesn't explain the spiritual significance of the precious metals and stones used in his illustration in 1 Corinthians 3:12. However, elsewhere in Scripture gold is typically used to indicate the glory of God, as seen in the tabernacle (Exod. 25) and the temple (1 Kings 6:21–32). Silver is the metal of redemption (Lev. 27). And though the precious stones aren't itemized, there are many other things Christians can do with their talents, time, and treasure to fulfill the great commandment to love God and others (Matt. 22:36–40).

3. Erwin Lutzer, *Your Eternal Reward: Triumph and Tears at the Judgment Seat of Christ* (Chicago: Moody Publishers, 2015), 51.

4. Norman Geisler, as quoted in Rhodes, *Wonder of Heaven*, 189 (emphasis in original).

5. William Barclay, *The Letters to the Philippians, Colossians and Thessalonians*, Daily Bible Series (Louisville: Westminster John Knox Press, 2003), 223.

6. Billy Graham, *Where I Am: Heaven, Eternity, and Our Life Beyond* (Nashville: W Publishing Group, 2015), 229.

7. John Walvoord, "End Times: Understanding Today's World Events in Biblical Prophecy," in *Understanding Christian Theology*, ed. Charles R. Swindoll and Roy B. Zuck (Nashville: Thomas Nelson, 2003), 1279.

8. Lutzer, *Your Eternal Reward*, 78.

Chapter 9 Who Will Be in Heaven?

1. See Leviticus 11:44–45; 19:2; 20:7, 26.

2. My book *Not All Roads Lead to Heaven: Sharing an Exclusive Jesus in an Inclusive World* (Grand Rapids: Baker Books, 2016) is dedicated to the exclusivity of Jesus Christ as the only means of salvation and way to heaven.

3. Lewis, *Mere Christianity*, 52.

4. On the exclusivity of Jesus as the source of salvation and means to heaven, see John 3:16; 11:25–26; Acts 16:31; Romans 10:9.

5. Charles R. Swindoll, *The Owner's Manual for Christians: The Essential Guide for a God-Honoring Life* (Nashville: Thomas Nelson, 2009), 229 (emphasis in original).

6. See Charles C. Ryrie, *Basic Theology: A Popular Systematic Guide to Understanding Biblical Truth* (Chicago: Moody, 1999), 37–38.

7. For a more in-depth discussion of what happens to children and the childlike when they die, see my book *Not All Roads Lead to Heaven*, 165–76.

Chapter 10 How Can I Prepare for My Journey to Heaven?

1. Warren Buffet, as quoted in Elliot Blair Smith, "Warren Buffet Signs Over $30.7 Billion to the Bill and Melinda Gates Foundation," *USA Today*, June 26, 2006, http://usatoday30.usatoday.com/money/2006-06-25-buffett-charity_x.htm.

2. George Marsden, *Jonathan Edwards: A Life* (New Haven, CT: Yale University Press, 2003), 51.

3. Jonathan Edwards, "The Christian Pilgrim," in *The Works of Jonathan Edwards*, vol. 2, ed. Edward Hickman (Edinburgh: Banner of Truth, 1974), 244.

4. Jonathan Edwards, *Jonathan Edwards' Resolutions and Advice to Young Converts*, ed. Stephen J. Nichols (Phillipsburg, NJ: Presbyterian and Reformed, 2001), 18–19, 24.

5. Winston S. Churchill, as quoted in James C. Humes, *The Wit and Wisdom of Winston Churchill: A Treasury of More than 1,000 Quotations and Anecdotes* (New York: HarperCollins, 1994), 25.

6. Adapted from Alcorn, *Heaven*, 457.

7. Henry David Thoreau, *Walden, or Life in the Woods* (New York: Everyman's Library, 1910), 80–81.

8. Ibid., 80.

9. John Greenleaf Whittier, "Maud Muller," in *The Poems of John Greenleaf Whittier* (Boston: James R. Osgood and Co., 1878), 206.

10. Bronnie Ware, "Regrets of the Dying," *Inspiration and Chai* (blog), November 19, 2009, http://bronnieware.com/regrets-of-the-dying/.

11. Audrey Hindle, "A Husband's Final Gift," as quoted in Robert Jeffress, *The Road Most Traveled: Releasing the Power of Contentment in Your Life* (Nashville: Broadman & Holman, 1996), 160–62.

12. As quoted in Charles R. Swindoll, *Living on the Ragged Edge: Coming to Terms with Reality* (Waco: Word, 1985), 358–59.

About the Author

Dr. Robert Jeffress is senior pastor of the 13,000-member First Baptist Church, Dallas, Texas, and a Fox News contributor. He is also an adjunct professor at Dallas Theological Seminary. Dr. Jeffress has made more than two thousand guest appearances on various radio and television programs and regularly appears on major mainstream media outlets such as Fox News channel's *Fox and Friends*, *The O'Reilly Factor*, *Hannity*, *Lou Dobbs Tonight*, *Varney and Co.*, and *Judge Jeanine*; ABC's *Good Morning America*; and HBO's *Real Time with Bill Maher*. Dr. Jeffress hosts a daily radio program, *Pathway to Victory*, that is heard nationwide on over eight hundred stations in major markets such as Dallas–Fort Worth, New York City, Chicago, Los Angeles, Washington, DC, Houston, and Seattle. His weekly television program can be seen in 195 countries and on 11,283 cable and satellite systems throughout the world, including China, and on the Trinity Broadcasting Network and Daystar.

Dr. Jeffress is the author of over twenty books, including *When Forgiveness Doesn't Make Sense*, *Countdown to the*

Apocalypse, and *Not All Roads Lead to Heaven*. Dr. Jeffress recently led his congregation in the completion of a $135 million re-creation of its downtown campus. The project is the largest in modern church history and serves as a "spiritual oasis" covering six blocks of downtown Dallas.

Dr. Jeffress has a DMin from Southwestern Baptist Theological Seminary, a ThM from Dallas Theological Seminary, and a BS from Baylor University. In May 2010 he was awarded a Doctor of Divinity degree from Dallas Baptist University, and in June 2011 he received the Distinguished Alumnus of the Year award from Southwestern Baptist Theological Seminary.

Dr. Jeffress and his wife, Amy, have two daughters, Julia and Dorothy, and a son-in-law, Ryan Sadler.

A PLACE CALLED
HEAVEN

Complete DVD Teaching Set

Teaching set includes . . .

» A hardcover copy of A PLACE CALLED HEAVEN

» The complete, unedited series on DVD

» A comprehensive instructor's guidebook, complete with answers
to study questions and expanded responses to key points

NOT ALL ROADS LEAD TO HEAVEN

Complete DVD Teaching Set

Teaching set includes . . .

» A hardcover copy of NOT ALL ROADS LEAD TO HEAVEN

» The complete, unedited nine-message series on DVD

» A CD-ROM with printer-friendly message notes and study questions for Sunday school classes and small groups

» A comprehensive instructor's guidebook, complete with answers to study questions and expanded responses to key points

ORDER NOW

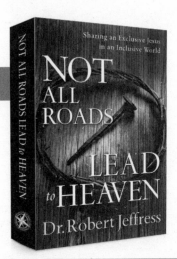

DR. ROBERT JEFFRESS
Pathway
ᴛᴏ Victory

ptv.org | 866.999.2965

Connect with

Relevant. Intelligent. Engaging.

Sign up for announcements about
new and upcoming titles at

www.bakerbooks.com/signup

 ReadBakerBooks

 ReadBakerBooks